Comprehensive CSS3 Command List, With Descriptions And Typical Mark Up

By
Online Trainees

ISBN-13: 978-1497370371

ISBN-10: 149737037X

Content

7

CSS Syntax

A CSS rule has two main parts: a selector, and one or more declarations:

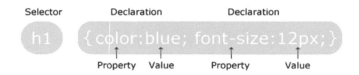

The selector is normally the HTML element you want to style.

Each declaration consists of a property and a value.

The property is the style attribute you want to change. Each property has a value.

P { margin :10px 10px 10px 10px }

Top   Right   Bottom   Left

ACCELERATOR

This property is specific to Microsoft. Microsoft, has the ability to turn off its system underlines for accelerator keys until the ALT key is pressed.

While this works for underlined elements (the HTML "U" element), it also seems to work for any element, although a different pseudo-underline color seems to be generated in such cases.

Mark up

u{accelerator:true}

<u style="accelerator:true">Underline></u>only first word

10

BACKGROUND

This is a shorthand property for setting all background properties in one declaration.

Inherited: No

Mark up

Option 1 – body {background: #FF0000}

Option 2 – body {background: url(test.gif) no-repeat top}

Option 3 – body {background: #00FF00 url(test.gif no-repeat fixed top}

Possible Values

Value

Background-color

Background-image

Background-repeat

Background-attachment

Background-position

BACKGROUND-COLOR

The background-color property sets the background color of an element.

Inherited: No

Mark up

p {background-color: #00ff00}

Possible Values

Color - Value can be a color name (red), a rgb value (rgb(255,0,0)), or a hex number (#ff0000)

Transparent - background color is transparent

BACKGROUND-POSITION

The background-position property sets the starting position of a background image.

Inherited: No

Mark up

body{background-image: url(test.gif); background-repeat: no-repeat;background position: top left}

body{background-image: url(test.gif);background-repeat: no-repeat; background-position: 0% 0%}

Possible Values

If only one keyword is used, the next will be center

top left

top center

top right

center left

center center

center right

bottom left

bottom center

bottom right

x-%y-%

x-pos y-pos

BACKGROUND-POSITION-X

If a 'background-image' is specified, this property specifies the initial position on the X-axis of the background image. A minimum value for this property indicates the left side of the rendering box, and a maximum value is at the right side. The Y-axis component of the background position can be specified using the 'background', 'background-position' or 'background-position-y' properties.

Mark up

div.marked {background-image: url(test.jpg);background-position-x: center}

Possible Values

[Percentage] - Percentage is in reference to the dimensions of the box of the current element. Value specifies the percentage on BOTH the image and the canvas and may be negative (eg: 20% indicates the reference point 20% from the left side of the image is to be located at 20% from the left side of the element's rendering box

[Length] - Represents an absolute X-coordinate position for the image and may be negative. Standard Absolute or Relative Length Units may be used here

left|center|right - Keywords representing X-axis screen positions for image placement

BACKGROUND-POSITION-Y

When a 'background-image' is specified, this property specifies the initial position on the Y-axis of the background image specified in the browser window if it is not continuously tiled in the element's rendering box. A minimum value for this property indicates the upper side of the rendering box, and a maximum value is at the lower side. The X-axis component of the background position can be specified using the 'background', 'background-position' or 'background-position-x' properties.

Mark up

body{ background-image: url(test.gif);background-repeat: repeat-x;background-position-y: bottom}

Possible Values

[Percentage] - Percentage is in reference to the dimensions of the box of the current element. Value specifies the percentage on BOTH the image and the canvas and may be negative (eg: 70% indicates the reference point 70% from the top side of the image is to be located at 70% from the top side of the element's rendering box

[Length] - Represents an absolute Y-coordinate position for the image and may be negative. Standard Absolute or Relative Length Units may be used here

tom|middle|bottom - Keywords representing Y-axis screen positions for image placement

BACKGROUND-REPEAT

The background-repeat property sets how a background image will be repeated.

Inherited: No

Mark up

body {background-image: url(test.gif);background-repeat: repeat-x}

Possible Values

repeat - The background image will be repeated vertically and horizontally

repeat-x - The background image will be repeated horizontally

repeat-y - The background image will be repeated vertically

no-repeat - The background-image will be displayed only once

BEHAVIOR

The Behavior property specifies one or more space separated URLs indicating script(s) to attach to a CSS selector. Behaviors allow the default functionality of a given element to be extended. Using simple CSS syntax that allows script to be separated from style and content, CSS behaviors offer a fairly elegant and efficient way to re-use script code.

Mark up

blockquote { behavior: url(test.htc) url(#behaveBinObject) }

<blockquote style="behavior: url(hilight.htc) url(#behaveBinObject)">Some text here</blockquote>

Possible Values

[Script URL] - Provides an absolute or relative URL reference to the Behavior.

[#Object ID] - The Behavior is a binary implementation. This syntax consists of a hash sign ("#") followed by an OBJECT element ID within the document that instantiates the binary implementation.

[Default Behavior] - Quite a few default behaviors ship with Internet Explorer 5.0. This syntax allows each default behavior to be easily referenced.

BORDER

This is a shorthand property which allows an author to specify the border-width, border-style, and border-color for all the borders of an element's rendering box at once. Unlike the 'margin' and 'padding' properties, this property cannot specify different values for each side. To do this, use the properties for each side instead ('border-top', 'border-right', 'border-bottom' and 'border-left'.)

Mark up

blockquote { border: medium dashed #ff0000 }

<blockquote style="border: medium dashed #ff0000">Some text here text</blockquote>

Possible Values

inherit - Explicitly sets the value of this property to that of the parent.

[border-width] - Uses a [border-width] value to render the border for an element's rendering box.

[border-style] - Uses a [border-style] value to render the border for an element's rendering box.

[border-color] - Uses a [border-color] value to render the border for an element's rendering box.

BORDER-BOTTOM

This is a shorthand property which allows an author to specify the border-width, border-style, and border-color for the bottom border of an element. If no color is specified, the value will be taken from the 'color' property.

16

Mark up

div.out { border-bottom: 10px outset #ffffff }
this is a test

Possible Values

inherit - Explicitly sets the value of this property to that of the parent.

[border-width] - Uses a [border-width] value to render the bottom border for an element.

[border-style] - Uses a [border-style] value to render the bottom border for an element.

[border-color] - Uses a [border-color] value to render the bottom border for an element.

BORDER-BOTTOM-COLOR

This property controls the color of the bottom border of an element's rendering box. If no border-color is specified for an element's border, the value of the 'color' property is used instead.

Mark up

div { border-bottom-color: green }

this is green

Possible Values

inherit - Explicitly sets the value of this property to that of the parent.

transparent - The border is transparent (with any accompanying 'border-width' thickness) – eg: elements below it shine through.

17

[color] - Sets the border to the indicated color value.

BORDER-BOTTOM-STYLE

This property controls the line style of the bottom border of an element's rendering box. Browsers that support this property are allowed to treat values of dotted, dashed, groove, ridge, inset, outset and double as the value solid.

Mark up

strong { border-bottom-style: groove }

this is a test

Possible Values

inherit - Explicitly sets the value of this property to that of the parent.

none - No border is rendered. This overrides any value of 'border-width', if present.

hidden - Creates the same effect as 'none'. Only difference is for border conflict resolution for table elements.

dotted - The border is rendered as a series of dots.

dashed - The border is rendered as a series of short lines.

solid - Renders a solid line.

solid - Creates the effect of the border being grooved or carved in the rendering surface (A 3-D groove – the opposite of 'ridge'.) The groove bevel color is rendered based upon the value of the 'color' property.

ridge - Creates the effect of the border being raised from the rendering surface (A 3-D ridge – the opposite of

18

'groove'.) The ridge bevel color is rendered based upon the value of the 'color' property.

inset - Creates the effect of the border being embedded in the rendering surface (A 3-D inset.) The inset bevel color is rendered based upon the value of the 'color' property. A distinction exists between this value and 'groove'.

outset - Creates the effect of the border coming out of the rendering surface (A 3-D outset – the opposite of 'inset'.) The outset bevel color is rendered based upon the value of the 'color' property. A distinction exists between this value and 'ridge'.

double - A double line drawn on top of the background of the element. The two lines with the space between adds up to the value of the 'border-width' property.

BORDER-BOTTOM-WIDTH

This property controls the thickness (width) of the bottom border of an element's rendering box. Negative values are not allowed.

Mark up

strong { border-bottom-width: medium }

this is a test

Possible Values

inherit - Explicitly sets the value of this property to that of the parent.

thin | medium | thick - Renders a "thin", "medium" or "thick" border on the bottom side of the element's rendering box. The actual thickness of these border values is not specified, but "thin" should have a smaller thickness

19

than "medium", which should have a smaller thickness than "thick".

[length] - Sets the width of the border on the bottom side of the element's rendering box to an explicit measurement.

BORDER-COLLAPSE

The rendering of table borders is divided into two categories – "collapsed" and "separated".

This property specifies which border rendering mode to use.

In the collapsed border model, adjacent table cells share borders.

In the separated model, adjacent cells each have their own distinct borders.

In the collapsed border model, provision is made for resolution of cases where borders specified for adjacent cells differ and are in conflict:

If any shared border has a component where the 'border' is set to "hidden" for ANY of the sharing members, the common border should be unconditionally set to "hidden".

If any shared border has a component where the 'border' is set to "none", it can be overridden by any other border-sharing member carrying a renderable 'border' property value.

If ALL border-sharing members specify a value of "none" for a border component, only then will the border be set to "none".

If a shared border has a 'border-width' contention, (with no component having a 'border' value of "hidden" of course…), the largest border-width should be rendered.

If a shared border has a 'border-style' contention, the suggested priority should be used (decreasing from left to right): "double", "solid", "dashed", "dotted", "ridge", "outset", "groove", "inset."

If a shared border has a 'border-color' contention, the suggested priority should be used (decreasing from left to right): Table cell, table row, row group, column, column group, table.

Mark up

table { border: medium double red; border-collapse: separate; border-spacing: 9pt 4pt }
<table style="border: medium double blue; border-collapse: separate; border-spacing: 9pt 4pt">

Possible Values

inherit - Explicitly sets the value of this property to that of the parent

collapse - Use the "collapsed borders" rendering model

separate - Use the "separated borders" rendering model

BORDER-COLOR

This is a shorthand property which allows an author to specify 'border-top-color', 'border-right-color', 'border-bottom-color', and 'border-left-color' properties using a single property and value notation (the values are given in this order separated by spaces.)

If one or more of the values are not present, the value for a missing side is taken from the opposite side that is present. If only one value is listed, it applies to all sides. If no border-color is specified for an element's border, the value of the 'color' property is used instead.

Mark up

21

em { border-color: blue }
this is an emphasized test

Possible Values

inherit - Explicitly sets the value of this property to that of the parent.

transparent - The border is transparent (with any accompanying 'border-width' thickness) – eg: elements below it shine through.

[color] - Sets the border to the indicated color value.

BORDER-LEFT

This is a shorthand property which allows an author to specify the border-width, border-style, and border-color for the left border of an element. If no color is specified, the value will be taken from the 'color' property.

Mark up

div.out { border-left: 10px outset #ffffff }

this is a test

Possible Values

inherit - Explicitly sets the value of this property to that of the parent.

[border-width] - Uses a [border-width] value to render the left border for an element.

[border-style] - Uses a [border-style] value to render the left border for an element.

[border-color] - Uses a [border-color] value to render the left border for an element.

BORDER-LEFT-COLOR

This property controls the color of the left border of an element's rendering box. If no border-color is specified for an element's border, the value of the 'color' property is used instead.

Mark up

div { border-left-color: green }

this is green

Possible Values

inherit – Explicitly sets the value of this property to that of the parent.

transparent - The border is transparent (with any accompanying 'border-width' thickness) – eg: elements below it shine through.

[color] - Sets the border to the indicated color value.

BORDER-LEFT-STYLE

This property controls the line style of the left border of an element's rendering box. Browsers that support this property are allowed to treat values of dotted, dashed, groove, ridge, inset, outset and double as the value solid.

Mark up

strong { border-left-style: groove }

this is a test

Possible Values

inherit - Explicitly sets the value of this property to that of the parent.

none - No border is rendered. This overrides any value of 'border-width', if present.

hidden - Creates the same effect as 'none'. Only difference is for border conflict resolution for table elements.

dotted - The border is rendered as a series of dots.

dashed - The border is rendered as a series of short lines.

solid - Renders a solid line.

solid - Creates the effect of the border being grooved or carved in the rendering surface (A 3-D groove – the opposite of 'ridge'.) The groove bevel color is rendered based upon the value of the 'color' property.

ridge - Creates the effect of the border being raised from the rendering surface (A 3-D ridge – the opposite of 'groove'.) The ridge bevel color is rendered based upon the value of the 'color' property.

inset - Creates the effect of the border being embedded in the rendering surface (A 3-D inset.) The inset bevel color is rendered based upon the value of the 'color' property. A distinction exists between this value and 'groove'.

outset - Creates the effect of the border coming out of the rendering surface (A 3-D outset – the opposite of 'inset'.) The outset bevel color is rendered based upon the value of the 'color' property. A distinction exists between this value and 'ridge'.

double - A double line drawn on top of the background of the element. The two lines with the space between adds up to the value of the 'border-width' property.

BORDER-LEFT-WIDTH

This property controls the thickness (width) of the left border of an element's rendering box. Negative values are not allowed.

Mark up

strong { border-left-width: 5mm }

this is a test

Possible Values

inherit - Explicitly sets the value of this property to that of the parent.

thin | medium | thick - Renders a "thin", "medium" or "thick" border on the left side of the element's rendering box. The actual thickness of these border values is not specified, but "thin" should have a smaller thickness than "medium", which should have a smaller thickness than "thick".

[length] - Sets the width of the border on the left side of the element's rendering box to an explicit measurement.

BORDER-RIGHT

This is a shorthand property which allows an author to specify the border-width, border-style, and border-color for the right border of an element. If no color is specified, the value will be taken from the 'color' property.

Mark up

div.out { border-right: 10px outset #ffffff }

this is a test

Possible Values

inherit - Explicitly sets the value of this property to that of the

[border-width] - Uses a [border-width] value to render the right border for an element.

[border-style] - Uses a [border-style] value to render the right border for an element.

[border-color] - Uses a [border-color] value to render the right border for an element.

BORDER-RIGHT-COLOR

This property controls the color of the top border of an element's rendering box. If no border-color is specified for an element's border, the value of the 'color' property is used instead.

Mark up

div { border-right-color: green }

this is green

Possible Values

inherit- Explicitly sets the value of this property to that of the parent.

transparent - The border is transparent (with any accompanying 'border-width' thickness) – eg: elements below it shine through.

[color] - Sets the border to the indicated color value

BORDER-RIGHT-STYLE

This property controls the line style of the right border of an element's rendering box. Browsers that support this property are allowed to treat values of dotted, dashed, groove, ridge, inset, outset and double as the value solid.

Mark up

strong { border-right-style: groove }

this is a test

Possible Values

inherit - Explicitly sets the value of this property to that of the parent.

none - No border is rendered. This overrides any value of 'border-width', if present.

hidden - Creates the same effect as 'none'. Only difference is for border conflict resolution for table elements.

dotted - The border is rendered as a series of dots.

dashed - The border is rendered as a series of short lines.

solid - Renders a solid line.

solid - Creates the effect of the border being grooved or carved in the rendering surface (A 3-D groove – the opposite of 'ridge'.) The groove bevel color is rendered based upon the value of the 'color' property.

ridge - Creates the effect of the border being raised from the rendering surface (A 3-D ridge – the opposite of 'groove'.) The ridge bevel color is rendered based upon the value of the 'color' property.

inset - Creates the effect of the border being embedded in the rendering surface (A 3-D inset.) The inset bevel color is rendered based upon the value of the 'color' property. A distinction exists between this value and 'groove'.

outset - Creates the effect of the border coming out of the rendering surface (A 3-D outset – the opposite of 'inset'.) The outset bevel color is rendered based upon the value of the 'color' property. A distinction exists between this value and 'ridge'.

double - A double line drawn on top of the background of the element. The two lines with the space between adds up to the value of the 'border-width' property.

BORDER-RIGHT-WIDTH

This property controls the thickness (width) of the right border of an element's rendering box. Negative values are not allowed.

Mark up

strong { border-right-width: 10px }

this is a test

Possible Values

inherit - Explicitly sets the value of this property to that of the parent.

thin | medium | thick - Renders a "thin", "medium" or "thick" border on the right side of the element's rendering box. The actual thickness of these border values is not specified, but "thin" should have a smaller thickness than "medium", which should have a smaller thickness than "thick".

[length] - Sets the width of the border on the right side of the element's rendering box to an explicit measurement.

BORDER-SPACING

This property specifies the distance between the borders of adjacent table cells in the "separated borders" model. The space between table cells uses the background color/image specified for the explicit or assigned TABLE element.

Mark up

table { border: medium double red; border-collapse: separate; border-spacing: 10pt 5pt }

<table style="border: medium double red; border-collapse: separate; border-spacing: 10pt 5pt">

Possible Values

inherit – Explicitly sets the value of this property to that of the parent.

[length length] - Specifies an explicit border spacing. Listing one length value should assign the value to both horizontal and vertical spacing, while specifying two values should assign the first value to the horizontal spacing and the second value to the vertical spacing.

BORDER-STYLE

This is a shorthand property which allows an author to specify 'border-top-style', 'border-right-style', 'border-bottom-style', and 'border-left-style' properties using a single property and value notation (the values are given in this order separated by spaces.) If one or more of the values are not present, the value for a missing side is taken from the opposite side that is present. If only one value is listed, it applies to all sides.

Mark up

29

strong { border-style: groove inset solid none }

<strong style=”border-style: dotted”>this is a test</strong>

Possible Values

inherit - Explicitly sets the value of this property to that of the parent.

none - No border is rendered. This overrides any value of 'border-width', if present.

hidden - Creates the same effect as 'none'. Only difference is for border conflict resolution for table elements.

dotted - The border is rendered as a series of dots.

dashed - The border is rendered as a series of short lines.

solid - Renders a solid line.

solid - Creates the effect of the border being grooved or carved in the rendering surface (A 3-D groove – the opposite of 'ridge'.) The groove bevel color is rendered based upon the value of the 'color' property.

ridge - Creates the effect of the border being raised from the rendering surface (A 3-D ridge – the opposite of 'groove'.) The ridge bevel color is rendered based upon the value of the 'color' property.

inset - Creates the effect of the border being embedded in the rendering surface (A 3-D inset.) The inset bevel color is rendered based upon the value of the 'color' property. A distinction exists between this value and 'groove'.

outset - Creates the effect of the border coming out of the rendering surface (A 3-D outset – the opposite of 'inset'.) The outset bevel color is rendered based upon the value of the 'color' property. A distinction exists between this value and 'ridge'.

30

double - A double line drawn on top of the background of the element. The two lines with the space between adds up to the value of the 'border-width' property.

BORDER-TOP

This is a shorthand property which allows an author to specify the border-width, border-style, and border-color for the top border of an element. If no color is specified, the value will be taken from the 'color' property.

Mark up

div.out { border-top: 10px outset #ffffff }

this is a test

Possible Values

inherit – Explicitly sets the value of this property to that of the parent.

[border-width] – Uses a [border-width] value to render the top border for an element.

[border-style] – Uses a [border-style] value to render the top border for an element.

[border-color] - Uses a [border-color] value to render the top border for an element.

BORDER-TOP-COLOR

This property controls the color of the top border of an element's rendering box. If no border-color is specified for an element's border, the value of the 'color' property is used instead.

Mark up

div { border-top-color: green }

this is green

Possible Values

inherit - Explicitly sets the value of this property to that of the parent.

transparent - The border is transparent (with any accompanying 'border-width' thickness) – eg: elements below it shine through.

[color] - ets the border to the indicated color value.

BORDER-TOP-STYLE

This property controls the line style of the top border of an element's rendering box. Browsers that support this property are allowed to treat values of dotted, dashed, groove, ridge, inset, outset and double as the value solid.

Mark up

strong { border-top-style: groove }

this is a test

Possible Values

inherit - Explicitly sets the value of this property to that of the parent.

none - No border is rendered. This overrides any value of 'border-width', if present.

hidden - Creates the same effect as 'none'. Only difference is for border conflict resolution for table elements.

dotted - The border is rendered as a series of dots.

32

dashed - The border is rendered as a series of short lines.

solid - Renders a solid line.

solid - Creates the effect of the border being grooved or carved in the rendering surface (A 3-D groove – the opposite of 'ridge'.) The groove bevel color is rendered based upon the value of the 'color' property.

ridge - Creates the effect of the border being raised from the rendering surface (A 3-D ridge – the opposite of 'groove'.) The ridge bevel color is rendered based upon the value of the 'color' property.

inset - Creates the effect of the border being embedded in the rendering surface (A 3-D inset.) The inset bevel color is rendered based upon the value of the 'color' property. A distinction exists between this value and 'groove'.

outset - Creates the effect of the border coming out of the rendering surface (A 3-D outset – the opposite of 'inset'.) The outset bevel color is rendered based upon the value of the 'color' property. A distinction exists between this value and 'ridge'.

double - A double line drawn on top of the background of the element. The two lines with the space between adds up to the value of the 'border-width' property.

BORDER-TOP-WIDTH

This property controls the thickness (width) of the top border of an element's rendering box. Negative values are not allowed.

Mark up

strong { border-top-width: thin }

33

this is a test

Possible Values

inherit - Explicitly sets the value of this property to that of the parent.

thin | medium | thick - Renders a "thin", "medium" or "thick" border on the top side of the element's rendering box. The actual thickness of these border values is not specified, but "thin" should have a smaller thickness than "medium", which should have a smaller thickness than "thick".

[length] - Sets the width of the border on the top side of the element's rendering box to an explicit measurement.

BORDER-WIDTH

This is a shorthand property which allows an author to specify 'border-top-width', 'border-right-width', 'border-bottom-width', and 'border-left-width' properties using a single property and value notation (the values are given in this order separated by spaces.) If one or more of the values are not present, the value for a missing side is taken from the opposite side that is present. If only one value is listed, it applies to all sides.

Mark up

strong { border-width: thick thin }

this is a test

Possible Values

inherit - Explicitly sets the value of this property to that of the parent.

thin | medium | thick - Renders a "thin", "medium" or "thick" border for a side of the element's rendering box. The actual thickness of these border values is not specified, but "thin" should have a smaller thickness than "medium", which should have a smaller thickness than "thick".

[length] - Sets the width of the border for a side of the element's rendering box to an explicit measurement.

BOTTOM

This describes the vertical offset for the bottom edge of the absolutely positioned element box from the bottom edge of the element's containing block. For relatively positioned boxes, the offsets are relative to where the box would appear normally in the document flow. Positive values are above the parent block's bottom edge and negative values are below.

Mark up

h2 { display: block; position: absolute; top: 20px; right: 50px; bottom: 20px; left: 50px }

<h2 style="display: block; position: absolute; top: 20px; right: 50px; bottom: 20px; left: 50px">content</h2>

Possible Values

inherit - Explicitly sets the value of this property to that of the parent.

auto - Default offset in the regular layout of the page.

[length] - Refers to an absolute distance from the reference containing block. Negative values are allowed.

[percentage] - Refers to a percentage of the height of the parent containing block. If the parent containing block does not have an explicit value, this value is interpreted like containing block. If the parent containing block does not have an explicit value, this value is interpreted like 'auto'.

CAPTION-SIDE

This property specifies the position of elements with an intrinsic (HTML CAPTION elements) or assigned 'display' property value of "table-caption" in relation to the table rendering box they are assigned to. Alignment within the table caption is accomplished using the 'text-align' and 'vertical-align' properties.

Mark up

caption { caption-side: right }

<caption style="caption-side: right">Caption</caption>

Possible Values

inherit - Explicitly sets the value of this property to that of the parent.

top - The caption is positioned above the rendered table box.

bottom - The caption is positioned below the rendered table box.

left - The caption is positioned to the left of the rendered table box.

right - The caption is positioned to the right of the rendered table box.

CLEAR

This property specifies whether the current element allows floated elements occuring earlier in the document to float along its sides. The values for this property indicate which

36

sides of the element do not allow floating elements. If the current element has any floating sub-elements, the property does not apply to them.

Mark up

address { clear: both }

<address style="clear: both">some test</address>

Possible Values

inherit – Explicitly sets the value of this property to that of the parent.

none – No restriction is made on floating element placement behavior.

left - The current element is shifted such that the top edge of the top margin is below the bottom edge of any left-floated elements previously occuring in the document.

right - The current element is shifted such that the top edge of the top margin is below the bottom edge of any right-floated elements previously occuring in the document.

both - The current element is shifted such that the top edge of the top margin is below the bottom edge of any floated elements previously occuring in the document.

CLIP

A clipping area describes the portions of an element's rendering box that are visible (when an element's 'overflow' property is not set to 'visible'.)

Parent element clipping regions also apply to calculating a current element's clipping area; in cases where multiple clipping regions apply to an element, only the intersection of the multiple regions should be displayed.

Mark up

p { overflow: scroll; position: absolute; width: 50px; height: 50px; clip: rect(5px 40px 40px 5px) }

some formatted text

Possible Values

inherit - Explicitly sets the value of this property to that of the parent.

auto - The clipping region is the same size as the element's rendering box.

[shape] - rect([top] [right] [bottom] [left])

This syntax defines a rectangular area where [top], [right], [bottom], and [left] are offsets from each respective side of the element's rendering box. In the future, other clipping shapes may be allowed.

COLOR

The color property sets the color of a text.

Mark up

body {color: rgb(255,255,0)}

body {color: #ffffff}

body {color: red}

Possible Values

color - The color value can be a color name (red), a rgb value (rgb(255,0,0)), or a hex number (#ff0000).

38

CONTENT

This property automatically generates content to attach before/after a CSS selector (using the :before and :after pseudo-elements.) One or more keywords may be specified for this property, but the content does not actually exist in the document tree; it is generated "on-the-fly." The 'display' property is used with this property to specify the type of rendering box for the generated content.

Mark up

em:before { content: url("ding.wav") }

Possible Values

inherit - Explicitly sets the value of this property to that of the parent.

[string] - The content of the value will be used as the generated text.

[url] - An absolute or relative URL pointing to an embeddable object. If rendering of the file is not possible by the browser, it should be ignored.

[counter()counters()] - counter(name) | counter(name, list-style-type)

Generated text is produced using "name" (the name of the counter at the current point in the document tree), and "list-style-type" accepts one of the named values used for the 'list-style-type' property (default "list-style-type" for the counter() function is 'decimal'.)

counters(name, string) | counters(name, string, list-style-type)

All counters with the indicated "name" label at the current point in the document tree will become the generated text, separated by the specified string value. The counters are rendered using the "list-style-type" (one of the named values used for the 'list-style-type' property, default "list-style-type" for the counters() function being 'decimal'.)

open-quote close-quote - A quote of the indicated type is inserted as appropriate, taking its value from the 'quotes' property.

no-open-quote no-close-quote - A quote is not inserted for the open/close quote, but the quote nesting level is still incremented/decremented accordingly.

[attr(X)] - This syntax returns a string which is the unparsed value of the indicated element attribute (X) for the current CSS selector. If the specified attribute does not exist, an empty string should be returned. Case sensitivity of the attribute name should depend on the language in use (eg: XML is case sensitive while HTML is not.) If the system supports it, you can also supply a namespace prefix to narrow down the attribute selection as well, eg: "attr(foo|align)" where "foo" is the namespace prefix, and "align" is the attribute being selected in that namespace ONLY.

COUNTER-INCREMENT

The 'counter-increment' property acts like an incremented variable in a programming language – it specifies the amount to increment the specified counter by when the current CSS selector is encountered. The property lists one or more counter labels, each followed by an optional increment integer value (default increment is 1.) Negative integers and zero are also valid.

If a counter is incremented AND rendered using a single CSS selector (with the 'content' property and 'before:'/'after:' pseudo-elements), it should be incremented first, then rendered. If a single CSS selector both increments and resets a counter, it is reset, then incremented.

Mark up

h1:before {counter-increment: main-heading; counter-reset: sub-heading; content: "Section " counter(main-heading) ":" }

Possible Values

inherit – Explicitly sets the value of this property to that of the parent.

none – Suppresses incrementing counters for the current selector.

[identifier integer] - Specifies one or more counters and the amount to increment the counter by.

COUNTER-RESET

The 'counter-reset' property acts like a variable assignment in a programming language – it sets a new value for the specified counter whenever the current CSS selector is encountered. The property lists one or more counter labels, each followed by an optional integer reset value (default reset value is 0.)

If a counter is reset AND rendered using a single CSS selector (with the 'content' property and 'before:'/'after:' pseudo-elements), it should be reset first, then rendered. If a single CSS selector both increments and resets a counter, it is reset, then incremented.

Mark up

h1:before {counter-increment: main-heading; counter-reset: sub-heading; content: "Section " counter(main-heading) ":" }

Possible Values

inherit – Explicitly sets the value of this property to that of the parent.

none – Suppresses resetting of counters for the current selector.

[identifier integer] - Specifies one or more counters to reset and the values to reset each one to.

CUE

The 'cue' family of properties allows the attachment of key sounds (or "Auditory Icons" as the CSS spec refers to them) to elements. This allows an author to add distinguishing characteristics to semantic elements. 'Cue' is a shorthand property for setting both 'cue-before' and 'cue-after' property values. If two values are given, the first value is assigned to 'cue-before' and the second is 'cue-after'. If only one value is given, it applies to both properties. If loading of a URL fails, nothing should be played, but if the system does not have the ability to play it, the spec says the system should try to use some sort of cue (audio, visual or other.)

Mark up

strong { cue: url(sound.wav) url(sound2.wav) }

text

Possible Values

inherit – Explicitly sets the value of this property to that of the parent.

none – Play no sound before and after the element.

[uel] - Indicates the URL of a sound file to be played before and after the element. If loading of the indicated URL fails no sound will be played. If the referenced

resource is not a sound file, it should be ignored and the property should be treated as if the value were set to 'none.'

CUE-AFTER

The 'cue' family of properties allows the attachment of key sounds (or "Auditory Icons" as the CSS spec refers to them) to elements. This allows an author to add distinguishing characteristics to semantic elements. This property specifically references a sound to be played after the element has been aurally rendered. If loading of a URL fails, nothing should be played, but if the system does not have the ability to play it, the spec says the system should try to use some sort of cue (audio, visual or other.)

Mark up

strong { cue-after: url(sound.wav) }

text

Possible Values

inherit – Explicitly sets the value of this property to that of the parent.

none - Explicitly sets the value of this property to that of the parent.

[url] - Indicates the URL of a sound file to be played after the element. If loading of the indicated URL fails no sound will be played. If the referenced resource is not a sound file, it should be ignored and the property should be treated as if the value were set to 'none.'

CUE-BEFORE

The 'cue' family of properties allows the attachment of key sounds (or "Auditory Icons" as the CSS spec refers to them) to elements. This allows an author to add

43

distinguishing characteristics to semantic elements. This property specifically references a sound to be played before the element has been aurally rendered. If loading of a URL fails, nothing should be played, but if the system does not have the ability to play it, the spec says the system should try to use some sort of cue (audio, visual or other.)

Mark up

strong { cue-before: url(orchestralsneeze.wav) }

text

Possible Values

inherit – Explicitly sets the value of this property to that of the parent.

none – Play no sound before the element.

[url] - Indicates the URL of a sound file to be played before the element. If loading of the indicated URL fails no sound will be played. If the referenced resource is not a sound file, it should be ignored and the property should be treated as if the value were set to 'none.'

CURSOR

This property controls the type of cursor that is used when a pointing device is over an element. Accepts a comma separated list of the below values. Browsers should attempt to first use the cursor indicated on the left, working to the right until it has a cursor it can use.

Note: Although the CSS spec says that this property is inherited, there are some cases in browsers where it is not explicitly so.

Some elements that use a different default cursor (eg: hyperlinks, text entry elements) will override the parent cursor type by default unless explicitly set to "inherit".

Mark up

blockquote { cursor: help }

<blockquote style="cursor: help">This is some text</blockquote>

Possible Values

inherit – Explicitly sets the value of this property to that of the parent.

default – Browser default cursor. Often an arrow.

auto – Browser determines what cursor to display according to context.

[URL] – URL of a custom cursor to be used for the specified selector. If multiple URLs are listed for a cursor, the leftmost one is used. If that is not available, an attempt is made for the the next one indicated to the right, and so on. If none of the URL-defined cursors can be used, a generic cursor indicated at the end of the list is used.

n-resize - Used to indicate when an edge of a box is to be moved/re-sized. Values represent directions relative to up/north.

ne-resize - Used to indicate when an edge of a box is to be moved/re-sized. Values represent directions relative to up/north.

e-resize - Used to indicate when an edge of a box is to be moved/re-sized. Values represent directions relative to up/north.

se-resize - Used to indicate when an edge of a box is to be moved/re-sized. Values represent directions relative to up/north.

s-resize - Used to indicate when an edge of a box is to be moved/re-sized. Values represent directions relative to up/north.

sw-resize - Used to indicate when an edge of a box is to be moved/re-sized. Values represent directions relative to up/north.

w-resize - Used to indicate when an edge of a box is to be moved/re-sized. Values represent directions relative to up/north.

nw-resize - Used to indicate when an edge of a box is to be moved/re-sized. Values represent directions relative to up/north.

crosshair – Usually resembles a plus sign ('+').

pointer – Used to present an actively selectable element, such as a hyperlink.

move – Used to indicate when something is movable.

text – Used to indicate that content is selectable. Often represented using an I-bar.

wait – Used to indicate that the user must wait because the program is busy. Usually represented by an hourglass or clock.

help – Used to indicate that help is available for the element. Often represented as a question mark or balloon.

hand – Use a hand icon.

all-scroll – Use an up/down/left/right arrow with a dot in the middle. Used to indicate that content can be scrolled in any direction.

col-resize – Used to indicate that a column can be horizontally re-sized. Represented with a vertical bar in the middle of two arrows pointing in opposite left/right directions.

row-resize – Used to indicate that a row or item can be vertically re-sized. Represented with a horizontal bar in the middle of two arrows pointing in opposite up/down directions.

no-drop – Used to indicate that a dragged item cannot be dropped at the current cursor position. Represented as a hand next to a small circle with a slash through it.

not-allowed – Used to indicate that a requested action can not be performed. Represented as a circle with a slash through it.

progress – Indicates that a process is running in the background, which will not affect user interaction with the system. Represented as an arrow with an hourglass next to it.

vertical-text – Used to represent editable vertical content. Represented as a horizontal I-bar.

alias – Use a cursor to indicate a shortcut or alias to another object. Often represented as an arrow with a small curved arrow next to it.

cell – Used to indicate that one or more "cells" (as in a spreadsheet) may be selected. Often rendered as a thick plus-sign, possibly having a dot in the middle.

copy – Used to indicate that content will be copied. Often rendered as an arrow with a small plus next to it.

count-down – Used to indicate a "count-down" operation by a program.

count-up – Used to indicate a "count-up" operation by a program.

count-up-down – Used to indicate a program is "counting-up" and "counting-down" in succession operation in a program.

grab – Used to indicate that content is "grabbable". Often rendered as an open hand.

grabbing – Used to indicate that content is in the act of being "grabbed". Often rendered as a closed/clenched hand.

spinning – Used to indicate that processing is being done by the program. Slightly different from the 'wait' value – 'wait' should indicate that no user interaction with the program is possible while the cursor is in that state, whereas 'spinning' indicates that the user may still interact with the program. Sometimes rendered as a spinning, striped ball.

DIRECTION

Text in some languages flows from right to left, while many other languages flow from left to right.

There will inevitably be cases where left to right text and right to left content must be intermingled.

Unicode allows for a complex process of determining the directional flow of content based on properties of the characters and content, as well as explicit controls for language "embeddings" and directional overrides.

This algorithm should be used with bi-directional content as formatted by CSS. The 'unicode-bidi' and 'direction'

48

properties specify how document content maps to the Unicode algorithm.

The 'direction' property specifies the base direction (reading order) for text content in an element. It is also meant to control the directionality of table columns, text overflow and positioning of justified text.

Mark up

div { unicode-bidi: embed; direction: rtl }

Bidi content right to left

Possible Values

inherit – Explicitly sets the value of this property to that of the parent.

ltr – Text flow is left-to-right.

rtl - Text flow is right-to-left.

DISPLAY

This property specifies the type of rendering box used for an element.

In a language such as HTML where existing elements have well-defined behavior, default 'display' property values are taken from behaviors described in the HTML specifications or from the browser/user default stylesheet.

In languages where display behavior is not defined (like XML), the default value is 'inline'.

In addition to the many different allowed display box types, one other value, "none", allows the display of an element to be turned off; all child elements also have their display turned off.

49

The document is rendered as though the element did not exist in the document tree.

Mark up

p { display: block }

content

Possible Values

inherit - Explicitly sets the value of this property to that of the parent.

none - This value turns off the display of an element (it has no effect on layout); all child elements also have their display turned off unconditionally. The document is rendered as though the element did not exist in the document tree. To render an element box's dimensions in the document formatting scheme, yet have its contents be invisible, see the 'visibility' property.

inline - This causes the element to generate one or more inline element boxes.

bock - This causes the element to generate a block element box.

inline-block - This causes the element to generate a block element box that will be flowed with surrounding content as if it were an single inline box (behaving much like a replaced element would.)

list-item - This causes the element to generate a block box for the content and a separate list-item inline box.

maker - This causes an additional marker box to be generated along with the content box. Generated content using the :before and :after pseudo-elements with this display value will place content in the marker box. If a marker is used with another type of element, the value is treated as "in-line." The position of the marker will lie outside the block box.

cmpact - Depending on context, this value for the display property creates either an in-line or block level rendering box. In each case different CSS properties may apply to the compact element. In a block level context, the compact element is rendered in the left or right margin of the block element. The compact element participates in line-height calculations for the current line, and the 'vertical-align' property value is relative to the block element.

run-in - Depending on context, this value for the display property creates either an in-line or block level rendering box. In each case different CSS properties may apply to the run-in element. Properties for the run-in element are inherited from its parent element in the document tree, not from the block element box it participates in.

[table-header-group | table-footer-group] - These values cause the element to behave like the corresponding THEAD and TFOOT HTML table elements which these values take their name from.

table - These values cause the element to behave like the corresponding HTML table element which these values take their name from. The 'inline-table' value does not have a direct mapping in HTML.

inline-table - These values cause the element to behave like the corresponding HTML table element which these values take their name from. The 'inline-table' value does not have a direct mapping in HTML.

table-caption – These values cause the element to behave like the corresponding HTML table element which these values take their name from. The 'inline-table' value does not have a direct mapping in HTML.

table-cell - These values cause the element to behave like the corresponding HTML table element which these values take their name from. The 'inline-table' value does not have a direct mapping in HTML.

table-row|table-row-group - These values cause the element to behave like the corresponding HTML table element which these values take their name from. The 'inline-table' value does not have a direct mapping in HTML.

table-column|table-column-group - These values cause the element to behave like the corresponding HTML table element which these values take their name from. The 'inline-table' value does not have a direct mapping in HTML.

ELEVATION

In an optimal listening environment, the soundstage is considered to be parallel to the floor, with origin point at the listeners head. This property specifies the vertical angle off of the soundstage plane giving up/down angle references as a location for a referenced element. Zero degree references are forward on the soundstage plane, with positive angular values being upward, and negative values being downward. This property only describes the desired end-user effect and does not specify how it is produced.

Mark up

p.high { elevation: 45deg }

Some text

Possible Values

inherit - Explicitly sets the value of this property to that of the parent.

below - below: Same as '-90deg'

level - level: Same as '0deg'

above - above: Same as '90deg'

lower - Subtracts 10 degrees from the current absolute or inherited elevation.

higher - Adds 10 degrees to the current absolute or inherited elevation.

[angle] -

Specifies an angle, between '-90deg' and '90deg'. '0deg' references straight ahead/forward on the soundstage plane (level with the listener.) '90deg' is directly overhead while '-90deg' is directly below.

EMPTY-CELLS

In the "separated borders" model, this property specifies whether to render borders around cells with no visible content.

Content with a 'visibility' property value of "hidden" or certain whitespace characters (Unicode 09[tab], 0A[linefeed], 0D[Carriage Return], and 20[space]) are not considered to be "visible" content by themselves.

Mark up

td { empty-cells: hide }

<td style="empty-cells: hide"> </td>

Possible Values

inherit – Explicitly sets the value of this property to that of the parent.

show – Render the specified border style for cells that do not contain visible content.

hide - Do not render any specified border style for cells that do not contain visible content.

FILTER

This property creates an extensible mechanism allowing special visual effects to be applied to content.

There are currently three categories of filters – Visual filters and Reveal/Blend Transition filters. Multiple filters can be applied to a selector to produce interesting results, with the order of application often playing an important role in the final visual result. Current filters only apply in a visual context, but the extensibility of the property could allow for other capabilities.

Mark up

img { filter: blur(strength=50) flipv() }

```
<img src="image.gif" mce_src="image.gif" style="filter:
blur(strength=50) flipv()">
```

FLOAT

Floating elements are elements whose rendering boxes are shifted to the left or right side of the current line.

Content boxes that follow are rendered along the side of the floated element; down the right side of elements floated to the left, and down the left side of elements floated to the right.

This property controls this floating behavior, specifying an element float to the left, right, or not at all. For correct rendering, a floated element needs to have an intrinsic or assigned 'width' value.

Mark up

img.test { float: left }

<img src="image.gif" mce_src="image.gif" style="float: left">Some floating text.

Possible Values

inherit – Explicitly sets the value of this property to that of the parent.

none - The element box is not floated.

left – The current element box will be floated to the left. Subsequent content flows around it to the right, starting at the top of the element box If this value is given, the 'display' property for the current element is ignored, unless it has the value 'none'.

right - The current element box will be floated to the right. Subsequent content flows around it to the left, starting at the top of the element box If this value is given, the 'display' property for the current element is ignored, unless it has the value 'none'

FONT

With CSS you are given great control over the way your text is displayed. You can change the size, color, style, and more. You probably already know how to make text bold or underlined, but did you know you could resize the size of your font using percentages?

Mark up

p {font: 12px arial}

p {font: italic small-caps bold 12px arial}

p {font: oblique small-caps 900 12px/14px arial}

55

p {font: menu}

Possible Values

font style - Sets the properties for a font. The line-height value sets the space between lines. The value can be a number, a %, or a font size

font-variant - Sets the properties for a font. The line-height value sets the space between lines. The value can be a number, a %, or a font size

font-weight - Sets the properties for a font. The line-height value sets the space between lines. The value can be a number, a %, or a font size

font-size/line-height - Sets the properties for a font. The line-height value sets the space between lines. The value can be a number, a %, or a font size

font-family - Sets the properties for a font. The line-height value sets the space between lines. The value can be a number, a %, or a font size

caption - Defines the font that are used by captioned controls (like buttons, drop-downs, etc.)

icon - Defines the fonts that are used by icon labels

menu - Defines the fonts that are used by dropdown menus

message-box - Defines the fonts that are used by dialog boxes

status bar - Defines the fonts that are used by window status bars

FONT-FAMILY

Font families can be divided into two groups: serif and san serif. A san serif font does not include the small lines at

56

the end of characters, while a serif font does include these small lines. When choosing which kind you prefer, remember that studies have shown that sans serif fonts are much easier to read on a computer monitor as opposed to a serif font.

Mark up

body {font-family: courier, serif}

p {font-family: arial, "lucida console", sans-serif}

<p style="font-family: arial, 'lucida console', sans-serif">

Possible Values

family-name

generic-family

FONT-SIZE

You can manipulate the size of your fonts by using values, percentages, or key terms. Using values are useful if you do not want the user to be able to increase the size of the font because your site will look incorrect if they did so. Percentages are great when you want to change the default font, but do not want to set a static value

Mark up

body {font-size: x-large}

p {font-size: 10px}

Possible Values

xx-small – sets the font top xx small

x-small – sets the font to x small

small – sets the font to small

medium – sets the font to medium

large – sets the font to large

x-large – sets the font to x large

xx-large – sets the font to xx large

smaller - Sets the font-size to a smaller size than the parent element

larger – Sets the font-size to a larger size than the parent element

length - Sets the font-size to a fixed size

% - Sets the font-size to a % of the parent element

FONT-SIZE-ADJUST

Specifies an aspect value for an element that will preserve the x-height of the first-choice font. If the aspect value is high, the font will be legible when it is set to a smaller size.

Mark up

h2 {font-size-adjust: 0.58}

Possible Values

none – Do not preserve the font's x-height if the font is unavailable

number - Defines the aspect value ratio for the font

FONT-STRETCH

The font-stretch property is used to expand or contract (condense) the horizontal width of the font. The change is relative to the normal width of the font as displayed by the browser.

narrower

The narrower value contracts the font to the next smaller width.

wider

The wider value expands the font to the next larger width. The order descends from narrowest to widest in value. The normal value is the normal width of the font as displayed by the browser.

Mark up

h2 {font-stretch: ultra-condensed}

Possible Values

normal - Sets the scale of condensation or expansion to normal

wider - Sets the scale of expansion to the next expanded value

narrower - Sets the scale of condensation to the next condensed value

ultra-condensed

extra-condensed

condensed

semi-condensed

semi-expanded

expanded

extra-expanded

ultra-expanded

FONT-STYLE

CSS Font-Style is where you define if your font will be italic or not. Possible key terms are the following: italic, oblique, and normal.

Mark up

body {font-style: italic}

Possible Values

normal – The browser displays a normal font

italic – The browser displays an italic font

oblique - The browser displays an oblique font

FONT-VARIANT

CSS Font Variant allows you to convert your font to all small caps. Note: not every font supports CSS Font Variant, so be sure to test before you publish.

Mark up

p {font-variant: small-caps}

Possible Values

normal – The browser displays a normal font

small-caps - The browser displays a small-caps font

FONT-WEIGHT

If you want to control the weight of your font (its thickness), using font weight is the best way to go about it. We suggest that you only use font-weight in multiples of 100 (e.g. 200, 300, etc) because any less and you probably will not see any difference. The values range from 100(thin)-900(thick).

Mark up

p {font-weight: bold}

Possible Values

normal – Defines normal characters

bold – Defines thick characters

bolder – Defines thicker characters

lighter - Defines lighter characters

100 - Defines from thin to thick characters. 400 is the same as normal, and 700 is the same as bold.

200

300

400

500

600

700

800

900

HEIGHT

This property specifies the height of an element's rendering box for block-level and replaced elements (for other types of elements, height calculations are taken from their inherited or assigned 'line-height' value.)

If an element's computed height is greater than that specified by the 'height' property, the content will overflow the rendering box according to the 'overflow' property. Negative values for the 'height' property are not allowed.

In addition to the 'height' property, two other properties – 'min-height' and 'max-height' – place constraints on the allowed value for an element's rendering box height. The 'height' value is first computed without consideration for these other two properties. If the computed value is greater than the 'max-height' value or less than the 'min-height' value, the height is re-calculated using the 'max-height' or 'min-height' as the new 'height' value.

Mark up

img.class1 { height: 75px; width: 75px }

<img style="height: 75px; width: 75px" src="image.jpg" mce_src="image.jpg">

Possible Values

inherit - Explicitly sets the value of this property to that of the parent.

auto – The height is determinant on the values of other properties.

[length] - Refers to an absolute measurement for the computed element box height. Negative values are not allowed.

[percentage] - Refers to a percentage of the height of the containing element block. If a height is not explicitly given for the containing block, it should be treated like 'auto'

IME-MODE

This property controls the state of the state of an Input Method Editor (IME) for user text entry fields. An IME is used in Asian languages to assist in the creation of characters from a large character set, using an entry device that contains only a small subset or an entirely different set of characters than the larger character set.

Mark up

input { ime-mode: deactivated }

<input type="text" name="text1″ value="initial value" style="ime-mode: deactivated">

Possible Values

auto - No change is made to the current IME entry mode. This value has the same effect as not specifying the 'ime-mode' property.

active - The IME is initially enabled. All characters are then entered by default through the IME unless the user manually disables the IME.

inactive - The IME is initially disabled. The user may manually activate the IME.

deactivated - The IME is initially disabled and cannot be manually activated for the current field.

INCLUDE-SOURCE

This property inserts another document into the current document, replacing the current element's content. Any elements or CSS properties applied to or inherited by the current element are applied to the inserted content as well.

Mark up

```
div {

position: absolute;

top: 100px; left: 300px;

width: 200px; height: 200px;

border: thin solid black;

include-source:
url(http://www.anotherdomain.com/example.htm);

}
```

Possible Values

[url] - An absolute or relative URL pointing to a
document. If rendering of the document is not possible by
the browser, it should be ignored and the regular element
content be displayed instead.

LAYER-BACKGROUND-COLOR

This value sets the background-color for the entire region
of the current element. This proprietary property behaves
in Netscape the way the 'background-color' property
SHOULD behave, while the actual 'background-color'
behavior is buggy in this regard.

This property was invented to create the correct behavior.

The 'background-color' property only covers the content
area of an element's rendering box, and if a border is also
used, there is a slight gap (2-3 pixels) between the
'background-color' and the border area, where the
background-color of the parent element shines through.

The 'layer-background-color' covers the whole region
specified by the element, including the gap area occurring
for the 'background-color' property, and the entire

dimension of the element specified by the 'width' and 'height' properties. Since this property is only understood by Netscape, and it fixes other buggy behavior, specifying both this and the 'background-color' property with the same value seems like a good idea.

Mark up

div {

position: absolute;

top: 100px; left: 300px;

width: 200px; border: thin solid black;

background-color: blue; layer-background-color: blue;

}

<div STYLE="position: absolute; top: 100px; left: 300px; width: 200px; border: thin solid black;background-color: blue; layer-background-color: blue;">text block</div>

Possible Values

[color] – This is a representation of the values for Red/Green/Blue used to determine a final display color. Please see the section on Color Units for details on the various color specification schemes.

transparent - This specifies that the parent element background/image will shine through if one exists, else the system default background/image value is used.

LAYER-BACKGROUND-IMAGE

This value sets the background-image for the entire region of the current element. This proprietary property behaves in Netscape the way the 'background-image' property SHOULD behave, while the actual 'background-image'

65

behavior is buggy in this regard. This property was invented to create the correct behavior.

The 'background-image' property only covers the content area of an element's rendering box, and if a border is also used, there is a slight gap (2-3 pixels) between the background-image and the border area, where the surface of the parent element shines through.

The 'layer-background-image' covers the whole region specified by the element, including the gap area occurring for the 'background-image' property, and the entire dimension of the element specified by the 'width' and 'height' properties. Since this property is only understood by Netscape, and it fixes other buggy behavior, specifying both this and the 'background-image' property with the same value seems like a good idea.

Mark up

div {

position: absolute;

top: 100px; left: 300px;

width: 200px; border: thin solid black;

background-image: url(bg2.gif);

layer-background-image: url(bg1.gif);

}

< div STYLE='position: absolute; top: 100px; left: 300px; width: 200px; border: thin solid black; layer-background-image: url(bg1.gif);'>text block< /div>

Possible Values

66

[ur] – It can be either an absolute or relative URL. Please see the section on URL Units for details on how to indicate a URL within a Style Sheet

none - No image is used as the background for the element

LAYOUT-FLOW

This property controls the direction and flow of the content in an element. Its use is deprecated in favour of the 'writing-mode' property which accomplishes the same purpose.

Mark up

div { layout-flow: vertical-ideographic; }

Content rendered vertically

Possible Values

horizontal - Character glyphs flow one after another from the source content from left to right, starting from the top of the element's rendering box. When a new line is started, it starts below the previous line at the left-hand side of the element's rendering box. This is the layout mode used in most Roman-based documents.

Vertical-ideographic - Character glyphs flow one after another from the source content from top to bottom, starting from the right side of the element's rendering box. When a new line is started, it starts to the left of the previous line at the top side of the element's rendering box. Full-width characters are rendered with their top on the same side as the top of the rendering box, and half-width characters (select kana glyphs and western characters) are rendered rotated 90 degrees clockwise to the original rendering box's orientation. This layout mode is used in East Asian typography.

67

LAYOUT-GRID

Asian languages often employ page layout for characters to achieve better visual formatting using a one or two-dimensional grid. The 'layout-grid' property is a shorthand method used to set the 'layout-grid-mode', 'layout-grid-type', 'layout-grid-line', 'layout-grid-char', and 'layout-grid-char-spacing' properties using a single property notation.

Mark up

div { layout-grid: both loose 15px 15px 2cm }

Content

snapped to a layout grid

LAYOUT-GRID-CHAR

Asian languages often employ page layout for characters for better visual formatting using a one or two-dimensional grid. This property controls the size of the character grid for the layout of an element's text content when the 'layout-grid-mode' is set to 'line' or 'both'. Visually, this property has an effect similar to the 'line-height' property.

Mark up

div { layout-grid-mode: line; layout-grid-char: 12px }

Content snapped to a layout grid

Possible Values

none – No line grid is used.

auto – The largest character in the font for the current element is used to determine the character grid.

[length] – Refers to either an absolute measurement or a relative measurement based on the current element's font size.

[percentage] - The percentage is relative to the height/width of the parent element.

LAYOUT-GRID-CHAR-SPACING

Asian languages often employ page layout for characters for better visual formatting using a one or two-dimensional grid. This property controls the character spacing granularity when the 'layout-grid-mode' is set to 'char' or 'both', and the 'layout-grid-type' property is set to 'loose'. Visually, this property has an effect similar to the 'line-height' property.

Mark up

div { layout-grid-mode: both; layout-grid-type: loose; layout-grid-char-spacing: 15px }

Content snapped to a layout grid

Possible Values

auto – The largest character in the font for the current element is used to determine the character grid spacing.

[length] - Refers to either an absolute measurement or a relative measurement based on the current element's font size.

[percentage] - The percentage is relative to the height/width of the parent element.

LAYOUT-GRID-LINE

Asian languages often employ page layout for characters for better visual formatting using a one or two-dimensional grid. This property controls the grid length granularity when the 'layout-grid-mode' is set to 'line' or 'both'. Visually, this property has an effect similar to the 'line-height' property.

Mark up

div { layout-grid-mode: both; layout-grid-line: 10px }

Content snapped to a layout grid

Possible Values

none – No line grid is used.

auto – The largest character in the font for the current element is used to determine the character grid.

[length] - Refers to either an absolute measurement or a relative measurement based on the current element's font size.

[percentage] - The percentage is relative to the height/width of the parent element.

LAYOUT-GRID-MODE

Asian languages often employ page layout for characters to achieve better visual formatting using a one or two-dimensional grid. This property controls the type (if any) of the page layout grid to be used.

Mark up

div { layout-grid-mode: both; layout-grid-type: loose; layout-grid-char-spacing: 15px }

```
<div style="layout-grid-mode: both; layout-grid-type:
loose;layout-grid-char-spacing: 15px">Content snapped to
a layout grid</div>
```

Possible Values

both - Character (char) and line grid modes are enabled.
This value allows full grid layout for an element.

none – No layout grid is used.

line – Only a line grid is used for the element.
Recommended for inline elements.

char - Only a character grid is used for the element.
Recommended for block-level elements.

LAYOUT-GRID-TYPE

This property controls the type of layout grid used when
rendering an element's text content.

Mark up

```
div { layout-grid-mode: both; layout-grid-type: loose;
layout-grid-char-spacing: 15px }
```

```
<div style="layout-grid-mode: both; layout-grid-type:
loose;layout-grid-char-spacing: 15px">Content snapped to
a layout grid</div>
```

Possible Values

loose - Indicates the line-grid commonly used in Chinese
and Korean text display. Chinese characters, kana and
wide characters have the grid applied. All other characters
are rendered as if 'layout-grid-mode' was set to "none" or
"line". CSS properties and values that would otherwise
change the width of a character (such as 'text-align:
justify') are disabled.

strict - Indicates the line-grid used in Japanese text display. Narrow characters (except content from "cursive" fonts) get half the grid increment applied to wide characters. Wide characters receive a grid increment if no other width adjustment is used.

fixed - The type of line-grid used in mono-space layout. All characters receive and are centered within an equal grid spacing (except content from "cursive" fonts.) CSS properties and values that would otherwise change the width of a character (such as 'text-align: justify') are disabled.

LEFT

This describes the horizontal offset for the left edge of the absolutely positioned element box from the left edge of the element's containing block. For relatively positioned boxes, the offsets are relative to where the box would appear normally in the document flow. Positive values are to the right of the parent block's left edge and negative values are to the left.

Mark up

h2 { display: block; position: absolute; top: 20px; right: 50px; bottom: 20px; left: 50px }

<h2 style="display: block; position: absolute; top: 20px; right: 50px; bottom: 20px; left: 50px">content</h2>

Possible Values

inherit – Explicitly sets the value of this property to that of the parent.

auto – Default offset in the regular layout of the page.

[length] - Refers to an absolute distance from the reference containing block. Negative values are allowed.

[percentage] - Refers to a percentage of the height of the parent containing block. If the parent containing block does not have an explicit value, this value is interpreted like 'auto'.

LETTER-SPACING

Specify the exact value of the spacing between your letters. Letter-spacing works best when pixels are used to define the spacing.

Mark Up

p {letter-spacing: 12px}

p {letter-spacing: -0.5px}

Possible Values

normal – Defines normal space between characters

length - Defines a fixed space between characters

LINE HEIGHT

This property specifies the height of an in-line element box. If the 'line-height' value is greater than the value of the 'font-size' for the element, this difference (called the "leading") is cut in half (called the "half-leading") and distributed evenly on the top and bottom of the in-line box. In this manner, the content of an in-line element box is centered within the line-box (assuming no 'vertical-align' property is also set to change this behavior.) Negative values for this property are not allowed. This property is also a component of the 'font' shorthand property.

A few other rules govern line-height calculation:

If the computed value for the 'line-height' property is less than the computed 'font-size' for an in-line element box, fonts may 'bleed' (overflow) the element box.

If this property is set for a block-level element box that contains in-line elements, the value specifies the minimal height of each of the in-line boxes.

For in-line element boxed, this property specifies the height of the boxes generated by the element. For in-line replaced elements the height of the element box is given by the 'height' property instead of the 'line-height' property.

If an element box contains text in more than one font-size, the 'line-height' property should be determined using the largest font-size. This helps to create consistent baselines between adjacent line boxes.

Mark up

div.test { line-height: 160%; font-size: 10pt }

content

Possible Values

inherit – Explicitly sets the value of this property to that of the parent.

normal – Sets the line height to a 'reasonable' value relative to the element's font face. Browser dependent results. CSS2 recommends a computed value between 1.0 and 1.2.

[number] – This number is a multiplier to determine the line height as a factor of the current element font-size. To

[length] – This sets the 'line-height' to an explicit length value. Negative values are not allowed.

[percentage] - This number is also a multiplier (like [number]) used to determine the line height as a factor of the current element font-size. To determine the line height from the [percentage], multiply the current element computed 'font-size' by the [percentage]. Negative values are not allowed.

LINE-BREAK

The Japanese language has especially strict rules regarding the conditions and characters after which a line may be broken. This property controls whether or not this strict line-breaking behavior is used.

Mark up

div { line-break: strict }

Long bit of Japanese content that wraps at some point

Possible Values

normal – Normal line-breaking rules are applied to Japanese content

strict - Strict line-breaking rules are enforced for Japanese content.

LIST-STYLE

This shorthand property is used when the author wishes to change the default display characteristics of list-markers in HTML list structures. An author can specify location of the marker, a graphic to be used and/or a standard set of symbols. Keywords may come in any order, but using multiple keywords that control the same behavior is not allowed. If a [list-style-image] is specified for the list marker, it will be used in place of any [list-style-type] also specified. Nevertheless, a [list-style-type] should always be specified in the event the [list-style-image] can not be loaded. A value of 'none' for the 'list-style' property should set both 'list-style-type' and 'list-style-image' to 'none.'

Mark up

ul { list-style: square inside url(yourdomain.com/test.gif) }

<ul><li style="list-style: square inside url(http://www.another domain.com/example.gif)">content</li></ul>

Possible Values

inherit – Explicitly sets the value of this property to that of the parent

[list-style-type] – See the property page for 'list-style-type' for more details on syntax and allowed values

[list-style-position] – See the property page for 'list-style-position' for more details on syntax and allowed values

[list-style-image] - See the property page for 'list-style-image' for allowed values

LIST-STYLE-IMAGE

This property indicates a graphic to be used for the list markers in the list structure. This should override the default appearance of list-markers in the current HTML list structure. If a 'list-style-image' is given a value of 'none' or the URL can not be loaded, the 'list-style-type' will be used in its place. The 'list-style-type' should always be specified in the event the URL pointed to in 'list-style-image' can not be loaded

Mark Up

ul { list-style-image: url(http://www.yourdomain.com/example.gif) }

<ul><li style="list-style-image: url(http://www.anotherdomain.com/test.gif)">content</li></ul>

76

Possible Values

inherit – Explicitly sets the value of this property to that of the parent

none – No list-marker will be displayed for the list item

[url] - This value indicates the URL source for the list-marker graphic. It can be either an absolute or relative URL. If the graphic can not be loaded, whatever 'list-style-type' property is set will be used

LIST-STYLE-POSITION

This property determines how the list-marker is rendered in relation to the content of the list item

Mark up

ul { list-style-position: inside }

<ul><li style="list-style-position: inside">content</li></ul>

Possible Values

iherit – Explicitly sets the value of this property to that of the parent

otside – This specifies that all list item content will be rendered indented from the list-marker

iside - This renders wrapped content at a similar indentation level to the list-marker

LIST-STYLE-TYPE

This property is used when the author wishes to change the default appearance of list-markers in HTML list structures. If a 'list-style-image' property is also given and it has a value of 'none' or the URL can not be loaded, the 'list-style-type' property value will be used in its place. This property should always be specified in the event the URL pointed to in 'list-style-image' can not be loaded. If a value for this property is not understood, the value 'decimal' should be used

Mark up

ul { list-style-type: square }

<ul><li style="list-style-type: disc">some text</li></ul>

Possible Values

iherit - Explicitly sets the value of this property to that of the parent

none - No list-marker will be displayed for each list item

disc | circle | square - This specifies standard symbols to use as non-ordered list markers. For each successive list-item, the symbol will remain the same.

'disc': Solid bullet

'circle': Hollow bullet.

'square': Solid square.

decimal - This specifies a standard set of symbols to use as ordered list markers. The values increment with each successive list item using a numeric sequence, eg: decimal integers – 1, 2, 3, 4, 5,…

decimal-leading-zero - This specifies a standard set of symbols to use as ordered list markers. The values increment with each successive list item using a numeric sequence, eg: decimal integers padded by initial zeros – 01, 02, 03, 04, 05,…

lower-roman | upper-roman - This specifies a standard set of symbols to use as ordered list markers. The values increment with each successive list item using an alphanumeric sequence, eg:

lower-roman – i, ii, iii, iv, v,…

upper-roman – I, II, III, IV, V,…

lower-alpha | upper-alpha - This specifies a standard set of symbol systems to use as ordered list markers. The values increment with each successive list item using an alphabetic sequence, eg:

lower-alpha – a, b, c, d, e,…

upper-alpha – A, B, C, D, E,…

lower-greek | lower-latin | upper-latin - This specifies a standard set of symbol systems to use as ordered list markers. The values increment with each successive list item using an alphabetic sequence, eg:

lower-greek – [alpha], [beta], [gamma], [delta],…

lower-latin – lower case latin letters

upper-latin – upper case latin letters

armenian | georgian | Hebrew - This specifies a standard set of symbol systems to use as ordered list markers. The values increment with each successive list item using an alphabetic sequence, eg:

armenian – traditional Armenian numbering

georgian – traditional Georgian numbering

hebrew – traditional Hebrew numbering

cjk-ideographic | hiragana | katakana | hiragana-iroha | katakana-iroha - This specifies a standard set of symbol systems to use as ordered list markers. The values increment with each successive list item using an alphabetic sequence, eg:

cjk-ideographic – 'plain ideographic numbers'

hiragana – Japanese phonetic Hiragana ordering: a, i, u, e, o, ka, ki,…

katakana – Japanese phonetic Katakana ordering: a, i, u, e, o, ka, ki,…

hiragana-iroha – Japanese phonetic Hiragana ordering: i, ro, ha, ni, ho, he, to,…

katakana-iroha – Japanese phonetic Katakana ordering: i, ro, ha, ni, ho, he, to,…

MARGIN

This is a shorthand property which allows an author to specify 'margin-top', 'margin-right', 'margin-bottom', and 'margin-left' properties using a single property and value notation (the values are given in this order separated by spaces.) If one or more of the values are not present, the value for a missing side is taken from the opposite side that is present. If only one value is listed, it applies to all sides.

CSS margins are transparent and the background value of the parent element shines through. Negative values are allowed for each margin value of this property, which opens the way for text overlays to be created.

Mark up

body { margin: 5px 0px 2px 25px }

```
<body style="margin: 5px 0px 2px 25px">this is some
text</body>
```

Possible Values

inherit – Explicitly sets the value of this property to that of the parent.

auto – This value specifies that a value determined by the browser be used for this property.

[length] – Refers to either an absolute measurement or a relative measurement based on the current element's font size.

[percentage] – Refers to a percentage of the width of the current element's containing block.

MARGIN-BOTTOM

This property controls the size of the bottom margin of an element's rendering box. Negative values are allowed. Margins are transparent and the background value of the parent element shines through.

Collapsing margins: adjoining vertical margins between regular-flow elements may collapse; The larger of adjacent margin values is used. If the adjacent margins are all negative, the larger of the negative values is used. If positive and negative vertical margins are adjacent, the value should be collapsed thus: the largest of the negative margin values should be subtracted from the largest positive margin value.

Mark up

blockquote { margin-bottom: 3.0in }

```
<blockquote style="margin-bottom: 3.0in">This is some
text</blockquote>
```

81

Possible Values

inherit – Explicitly sets the value of this property to that of the parent.

auto – This value specifies that a value determined by the browser be used for this property.

[length] - Refers to either an absolute measurement or a relative measurement based on the current element's font size.

[percentage] - Refers to a percentage of the width of the current element's containing block.

MARGIN-LEFT

This property controls the size of the left margin of an element's rendering box. Negative values are allowed. Margins are transparent and the background value of the parent element shines through.

Collapsing margins: adjoining horizontal margins between elements should not collapse.

Mark up

h5 { margin-left: 1.0cm }

<h5 style="margin-legt: 3.0in">This is some text</h5>

Possible Values

inherit – Explicitly sets the value of this property to that of the parent.

auto – This value specifies that a value determined by the browser be used for this property.

[length] – Refers to either an absolute measurement or a relative measurement based on the current element's font size.

[percentage] - Refers to a percentage of the width of the current element's containing block.

MARGIN-RIGHT

This property controls the size of the right margin of an element's rendering box. Negative values are allowed. Margins are transparent and the background value of the parent element shines through.

Collapsing margins: adjoining horizontal margins between elements should not collapse.

Mark up

h1 { margin-right: auto }

<h1 style="margin-right: auto">This is some text</h1>

Possible Values

inherit – Explicitly sets the value of this property to that of the parent.

auto – This value specifies that a value determined by the browser be used for this property.

[length] – Refers to either an absolute measurement or a relative measurement based on the current element's font size.

[percentage] - Refers to a percentage of the width of the current element's containing block.

MARGIN-TOP

This property controls the size of the top margin of an element's rendering box. Negative values are allowed. Margins are transparent and the background value of the parent element shines through.

Collapsing margins: adjoining vertical margins between regular-flow elements may collapse; The larger of adjacent margin values is used. If the adjacent margins are all negative, the larger of the negative values is used. If positive and negative vertical margins are adjacent, the value should be collapsed thus: the largest of the negative margin values should be subtracted from the largest positive margin value.

Mark Up

address { margin-top: 33% }

<address style="margin-top: 33%">This is a test</address>

Possible Values

inherit - Explicitly sets the value of this property to that of the parent.

auto – This value specifies that a value determined by the browser be used for this property.

[length] – Refers to either an absolute measurement or a relative measurement based on the current element's font size.

[percentage] - Refers to a percentage of the width of the current element's containing block.

MARKER-OFFSET

In :before or :after pseudo-elements, the 'display' property can be set to "marker" to allow content to be paired with other content (usually iteratively, such as with the 'list-style-type' property behavior. An element's content creates a "principal" rendering box. The "marker" for the "principal" box should be formatted in a single-line outside the "principal" box. The "marker" box should allow the border and padding properties, but not margins.

The 'marker-offset' property gives a horizontal distance between the marker box and the "principal" rendering box, measured between the adjacent neighboring edges of the two boxes

Mark up

li:before { display: marker; marker-offset: 5px }

<ul><li style="marker-offset: 5px">this is some text</li></ul>

Possible Values

inherit – Explicitly sets the value of this property to that of the parent

auto – The browser determines the distance between the near edges of the marker box and the content box

[length] - A specified length value is used to determines the distance between the near edges of the marker box and the content box

MARKS

Printed documents in the printing industry often carry marks on the page outside the content area. These marks are used to align and trim groups of papers.

This property specifies what sort of marks should be rendered just outside the rendered page box. The characteristics and position of the marks will be browser dependent.

Mark up

body { marks: crop cross }

<body style="marks: crop cross">test text in the body</body>

Possible Values

inherit – Explicitly sets the value of this property to that of the parent.

none – No page marking will occur.

crop – Specifies that crop marks be used to indicate where the page should be cut.

cross - Specifies that cross-hair marks be rendered in order to precisely align the current page with other pages carrying 'cross' marks.

MAX-HEIGHT

This property allows a maximum height to be set for an element box. The calculation for the element's height may be less than this value, but if the calculated 'height' value is above this value it will recompute the 'height' using the 'max-height' value as the new 'height' value. If the value of 'min-height' is greater than the value of 'max-height', the 'max-height' property value becomes the 'min-height' value.

Mark up

h5 { max-height: 150px }

<h5 style="max-height: 150px">content</h5>

Possible Values

inherit – Explicitly sets the value of this property to that of the parent.

none – No limit is placed on the maximum allowable height for the element.

[length] – Refers to an absolute measurement for the maximum computed element box height. Negative values are not allowed.

[percentage] - Refers to a percentage of the height of the containing element block. If a value is not explicitly given for the containing block, it should be treated like 'auto'.

MAX-WIDTH

This property allows a maximum width to be set for an element box. The calculation for the element's width may be less than this value, but if the calculated 'width' value is above this value it will recompute the 'width' using the 'max-width' value as the new 'width' value. If the value of 'min-width' is greater than the value of 'max-width', the 'max-width' property value becomes the 'min-width' value.

Mark up

h5 { max-width: 150px }

<h5 style="max-width: 150px">content</h5>

Possible Values

inherit – Explicitly sets the value of this property to that of the parent.

none – No limit is placed on the maximum allowable width for the element.

[length] – Refers to an absolute measurement for the maximum computed element box width. Negative values are not allowed.

[percentage] - Refers to a percentage of the width of the containing element block.

MIN-HEIGHT

This property allows a minimum height to be set for an element box. The calculation for the element's height may be greater than this value, but if the value falls below this value it will recompute the height based on the 'min-height' value. If the value of 'min-height' is greater than the value of 'max-height', the 'max-height' property value becomes the 'min-height' value. If the calculated value for the 'height' property is less than the 'min-height' value, the calculations are done again using the 'min-height' value as the value for the 'height' property.

Mark up

h5 { min-height: 100px }

<h5 style="min-height: 100px">content</h5>

Possible Values

inherit – Explicitly sets the value of this property to that of the parent.

[length] – Refers to an absolute measurement for the minimum computed element box height. Negative values are not allowed.

[percentage] - Refers to a percentage of height of the containing element block. If a height is not explicitly given for the containing block, it should be treated like 'auto'.

MIN-WIDTH

This property allows a minimum width to be set for an element box. The calculation for the element's width may be greater than this value, but if the value falls below this value it will re-compute the width based on the 'min-width' value. If the value of 'min-width' is greater than the value of 'max-width', the 'max-width' property value becomes the 'min-width' value. If the calculated value for the 'width' property is less than the 'min-width' value, the calculations are done again using the 'min-width' value as the value for the 'width' property.

Additionally, the browser may have its own minimum allowable width for a specific element type. If the specified 'min-width' is less than this value for an element, the browser default minimum width may be used in its place.

Mark up

h5 { min-width: 100px }

<h5 style="min-width: 100px&quot>content</h5>

Possible Values

inherit – Explicitly sets the value of this property to that of the parent.

[length] – Refers to an absolute measurement for the minimum computed element box width. Negative values are not allowed.

[percentage] - Refers to a percentage width of the containing element block.

ORPHANS

This property specifies the minimum number of lines of content for the current element that must be left at the bottom of a page in a paged display environment.

Mark up

p { orphans: 4 }

test text in the paragraph

Possible Values

inherit – Explicitly sets the value of this property to that of the parent.

[integer] - Specifies an integer value representing the minimum number of lines of content that must be left at the bottom of a page.

OUTLINE-COLOR

The 'outline-color' property specifies a color for the outline for an element.

The outline properties create a uniform line around an object in order to draw visual attention. An outline is slightly different than a border in several ways: An outline is drawn starting "just outside the border edge" and is allowed to be non-rectangular. Outlines are always rendered on TOP of an element's rendering box and do not influence the box's position or size calculation; the document does not need to be re-flowed when a border is rendered or hidden, but the outline may overlap other nearby elements.

Mark up

img { outline-color: black }

<img src="image.gif" mce_src="image.gif" style="outline-color: green">

Possible Values

inherit – Explicitly sets the value of this property to that of the parent

invert – This value inverts the color of the outline to the opposite value of the color "underneath" the outline to ensure proper contrast

color - Sets the border to the indicated color value

OUTLINE-STYLE

The 'outline-style' property specifies an outline line style for the current element.

The outline properties create a uniform line around an object in order to draw visual attention. An outline is slightly different than a border in several ways: An outline is drawn starting "just outside the border edge" and is allowed to be non-rectangular. Outlines are always rendered on TOP of an element's rendering box and do not influence the box's position or size calculation; the document does not need to be re-flowed when a border is rendered or hidden, but the outline may overlap other nearby elements.

Mark up

button { outline-style: ridge }

<button style="outline-style: groove">Press Me!</button>

Possible Values

inherit - Explicitly sets the value of this property to that of the parent.

none - No border is rendered. This overrides any value of 'border-width', if present.

hidden - Creates the same effect as 'none'. Only difference is for border conflict resolution for table elements.

dotted - The border is rendered as a series of dots.

dashed - The border is rendered as a series of short lines.

solid - Renders a solid line.

solid - Creates the effect of the border being grooved or carved in the rendering surface (A 3-D groove – the opposite of 'ridge'.) The groove bevel color is rendered based upon the value of the 'color' property.

ridge - Creates the effect of the border being raised from the rendering surface (A 3-D ridge – the opposite of 'groove'.) The ridge bevel color is rendered based upon the value of the 'color' property.

inset - Creates the effect of the border being embedded in the rendering surface (A 3-D inset.) The inset bevel color is rendered based upon the value of the 'color' property. A distinction exists between this value and 'groove'.

outset - Creates the effect of the border coming out of the rendering surface (A 3-D outset – the opposite of 'inset'.) The outset bevel color is rendered based upon the value of the 'color' property. A distinction exists between this value and 'ridge'.

double - A double line drawn on top of the background of the element. The two lines with the space between adds up to the value of the 'border-width' property.

OUTLINE-WIDTH

The 'outline-width' property specifies the width for the outline of an element.

The outline properties create a uniform line around an object in order to draw visual attention. An outline is slightly different than a border in several ways: An outline is drawn starting "just outside the border edge" and is allowed to be non-rectangular. Outlines are always rendered on TOP of an element's rendering box and do not influence the box's position or size calculation; the document does not need to be re-flowed when a border is rendered or hidden, but the outline may overlap other nearby elements

Mark up

input { outline-width: thin }

<input type="text" name="text1" value="Default Text" style="outline-width: thin">

Possible Values

inherit – Explicitly sets the value of this property to that of the parent

thin | medium | thick - Renders a "thin", "medium" or "thick" outline border for the element's rendering box. The actual thickness of these outline values is not specified, but "thin" should have a smaller thickness than "medium", which should have a smaller thickness than "thick"

[length] - Sets the width of the outline around the current element rendering box to an explicit measurement

OVERFLOW

Some content in an element may fall outside the element's rendering box for a number of reasons (negative margins, absolute positioning, content exceeding the width/height set for an element, etc.) In cases where this occurs, the 'overflow' property describes what to do with the content outside the elements rendering area.

Mark up

blockquote { width: 50px; height: 50px; overflow: scroll }

<blockquote style="width: 50px; height: 50px; overflow: scroll">some text</blockquote>

Possible Values

inherit – Explicitly sets the value of this property to that of the parent.

visible – Content is not clipped and may be rendered outside of the element's box.

hidden – Content is not clipped and may be rendered outside of the element's box.

scroll – Content is clipped as necessary, but scrollbars are made available where necessary to view the additional, non-visible content. If the Visual media in use is static (such as Print) the content should be treated as if the value was 'visible'.

auto - This value is browser and media dependent, but should allow for a scrollbar if possible in case of overflow.

OVERFLOW-X

Some content in an element may fall outside the element's rendering box for a number of reasons (negative margins, absolute positioning, content exceeding the width/height set for an element, etc.) In cases where this occurs, the 'overflow-x' property describes what to do with the content that exceeds the element's width.

Mark up

blockquote { width: 50px; height: 50px; overflow-x: scroll }

<blockquote style="width: 50px; height: 50px; overflow-x: scroll">some text</blockquote>

Possible Values

visible – Content is not clipped and may be rendered outside of the element's box.

hidden – Content is clipped and content outside of the element's box is not visible. The size of the clipping region is defined by the 'clip' property.

scroll – Content is clipped as necessary, but a horizontal scrollbar is made available where necessary to view the additional, non-visible content. If the Visual media in use is static (such as Print) the content should be treated as if the value was 'visible'.

auto - This value is browser and media dependent, but should allow for a horizontal scrollbar if possible in case of overflow.

OVERFLOW-Y

Some content in an element may fall outside the element's rendering box for a number of reasons (negative margins, absolute positioning, content exceeding the width/height set for an element, etc.) In cases where this occurs, the 'overflow-y' property describes what to do with the content that exceeds the element's height.

Mark up

blockquote { width: 50px; height: 50px; overflow-y: scroll }

```
<blockquote style="width: 50px; height: 50px; overflow-
y: scroll">some text</blockquote>
```

Possible Values

visible – Content is not clipped and may be rendered outside of the element's box.

hidden – Content is clipped and content outside of the element's box is not visible. The size of the clipping region is defined by the 'clip' property.

scroll – Content is clipped as necessary, but a vertical scrollbar is made available where necessary to view the additional, non-visible content. If the Visual media in use is static (such as Print) the content should be treated as if the value was 'visible'.

auto - This value is browser and media dependent, but should allow for a vertical scrollbar if possible in case of overflow.

PADDING

This is a shorthand property which allows an author to specify 'padding-top', 'padding-right', 'padding-bottom', and 'padding-left' properties using a single property and value notation (the values are given in this order separated by spaces.) If one or more of the values are not present, the value for a missing side is taken from the opposite side that is present. If only one value is listed, it applies to all sides. The rendered surface of the padding area is taken from the 'background' property.

Mark up

```
body { padding: 5px 5px 2px 25px }

<body style="padding: 5px 5px 2px 25px">this is some
content</body>
```

Possible Values

inherit – Explicitly sets the value of this property to that of the parent.

[length] – Refers to either an absolute measurement or a relative measurement based on the current element's font size.

[percentage] - Refers to a percentage of the width of the current element's containing block.

PADDING-BOTTOM

This property controls the size of the bottom padding of an element's rendering box. Negative values are not allowed.

Mark up

blockquote { padding-bottom: 3em }

<blockquote style="padding-bottom: 3em">This is some text</blockquote>

Possible Values

inherit – Explicitly sets the value of this property to that of the parent.

[length] – Refers to either an absolute measurement or a relative measurement based on the current element's font size.

[percentage] - Refers to a percentage of the width of the current element's containing block.

PADDING-LEFT

This property controls the size of the left padding of an element's rendering box. Negative values are not allowed.

Mark up

blockquote { padding-left: 3em }

<blockquote style="padding-left: 3em">This is some text</blockquote>

Possible Values

inherit – Explicitly sets the value of this property to that of the parent.

[length] – Refers to either an absolute measurement or a relative measurement based on the current element's font size

[percentage] - Refers to a percentage of the width of the current element's containing block.

PADDING-RIGHT

This property controls the size of the right padding of an element's rendering box. Negative values are not allowed.

Mark up

blockquote { padding-right: 3em }

<blockquote style="padding-right: 3em">This is some text</blockquote>

Possible Values

inherit - Explicitly sets the value of this property to that of the parent.

[length] – Refers to either an absolute measurement or a relative measurement based on the current element's font size.

[percentage] - Refers to a percentage of the width of the current element's containing block.

PADDING-TOP

This property controls the size of the top padding of an element's rendering box. Negative values are not allowed.

Mark up

blockquote { padding-top: 3em }

<blockquote style="padding-top: 3em">This is some text</blockquote>

Possible Values

Inherit – Explicitly sets the value of this property to that of the parent.

[length] – Refers to either an absolute measurement or a relative measurement based on the current element's font size.

[percentage] - Refers to a percentage of the width of the current element's containing block.

PAGE

This property is used to specify a specific page type to use when displaying an element box. If the value specified is different than the one for the rendered element box that precedes it, one or two page breaks should be inserted between them, and the element box should then be rendered on a page box of the indicated type.

Mark up

@page doublepage { size: 8.5in 11in; page-break-after: left }

body { page: doublepage; page-break-after: right }

```
<body style="page: doublepage; page-break-after:
right">test text in the body</body>
```

Possible Values

auto – References the current default page.

[identifier] - Specifies an identifier for a page type defined in an @page rule.

PAGE-BREAK-AFTER

This property specifies the page-breaking behavior that should occur after an element box and on what side of the page the content that follows should resume on. Page breaks are not allowed in absolutely positioned elements.

Mark up

```
p { page-break-after: always }
```

```
<p style="page-break-after: always">Test text in the
paragraph</p>
```

Possible Values

inherit -

auto – Explicitly sets the value of this property to that of the parent.

avoid – Insert a page break before the element as necessary.

left|right – left: Force one or two page breaks after the current element box until a blank left page is reached.

right: Force one or two page breaks after the current element box until a blank right page is reached.

always – Always force a page break before the current element box.

{empty string] - No property value is used in this case. A page break is not inserted before the current element box.

PAGE-BREAK-BEFORE

This property specifies the page-breaking behavior that should occur before an element box and on what side of the page the content that follows should resume on. Page breaks are not allowed in absolutely positioned elements.

CSS2 "suggests" when page-breaking should occur:

Page-breaking should occur as few times as possible.

Page-breaking should be avoided inside these elements: tables, floated elements and block elements with borders.

Pages that are not forced to break should have approximately the same height.

Mark up

p { page-break-before: always }

Test text in the paragraph

Possible Values

inherit – Explicitly sets the value of this property to that of the parent.

auto – Insert a page break before the element as necessary.

avoid – Avoid inserting a page break before the current element box.

left|right – left: Force one or two page breaks before the current element box until a blank left page is reached.

right: Force one or two page breaks before the current element box until a blank right page is reached.

always – Always force a page break before the current element box.

{empty string] - No property value is used in this case. A page break is not inserted before the current element box.

PAGE-BREAK-INSIDE

This property specifies the page-breaking behavior that should occur inside an element's rendering box. Page breaks are not allowed in absolutely positioned elements.

Mark up

p { page-break-inside: auto }

Test text in the paragraph

Possible Values

inherit – Explicitly sets the value of this property to that of the parent.

auto – Insert page breaks inside the element box as necessary.

Avoid inserting page breaks inside the current element box if possible.

avoid -

PAUSE

This is a shorthand property used to set the 'pause-before' and 'pause-after' properties. If two values are given, the first refers to 'pause-before' and the second to 'pause-after'. If only one value is given, it is used for both properties.

Mark up

blockquote { pause: 2s 3s }

<blockquote style="pause: 2s 3s">text</blockquote>

Possible Values

inherit – Explicitly sets the value of this property to that of the parent.

[time] – Sets the pause length to a time measurement (see the time units for more details)

[percentage] - Refers to the inverse of the value of the 'speech-rate' property. (eg: a value of 100% for 'pause-after' with a 'speech-rate' of 60 words per minute would create a pause of 1 second.)

PAUSE-AFTER

This property specifies a pause to be inserted after speaking an element's content. The pause is inserted between the element's content and any 'cue-before' or 'cue-after' content.

Mark up

blockquote { pause-after: 1.5s }

<blockquote style="pause-after: 1.5s">text</blockquote>

Possible Values

inherit – Explicitly sets the value of this property to that of the parent.

[time] – Sets the pause length to a time measurement (see the time units for more details)

103

[percentage] - Refers to the inverse of the value of the 'speech-rate' property. (eg: a value of 100% for 'pause-after' with a 'speech-rate' of 60 words per minute would create a pause of 1 second.)

PAUSE-BEFORE

This property specifies a pause to be inserted before speaking an element's content. The pause is inserted between the element's content and any 'cue-before' or 'cue-after' content.

Mark up

blockquote { pause-before: 1.5s }

<blockquote style="pause-before: 1.5s">text</blockquote>

Possible Values

inherit – Explicitly sets the value of this property to that of the parent.

[time] – Sets the pause length to a time measurement (see the time units for more details)

[percentage] - Refers to the inverse of the value of the 'speech-rate' property. (eg: a value of 100% for 'pause-before' with a 'speech-rate' of 60 words per minute would create a pause of 1 second.)

PITCH

This property specifies the average frequency of the speaking voice. Different voice families have different average frequencies (a male voice is approx. 120Hz, a female voice is approx 210Hz.)

Mark up

strong { pitch: x-high }

content

Possible Values

inherit – Explicitly sets the value of this property to that of the parent.

x-low - These do not map to absolute frequencies since they are dependent on voice family. The obvious scale between values should be maintained no matter the voice family.

low - These do not map to absolute frequencies since they are dependent on voice family. The obvious scale between values should be maintained no matter the voice family.

medium - These do not map to absolute frequencies since they are dependent on voice family. The obvious scale between values should be maintained no matter the voice family.

high - These do not map to absolute frequencies since they are dependent on voice family. The obvious scale between values should be maintained no matter the voice family.

x-high - These do not map to absolute frequencies since they are dependent on voice family. The obvious scale between values should be maintained no matter the voice family.

[frequency] - Positive number indicating average voice pitch measured in Hertz or Kilohertz.

PITCH-RANGE

Meaning and emphasis is created in most languages by varying the pitch and inflection of the voice. This property specifies the degree of variation from the average pitch of

105

the voice being used to render the content. A voice with a small pitch-range will sound monotone, while a voice with high pitch range values will sound very animated.

Mark up

strong { pitch-range: 80 }

content

Possible Values

inherit – Explicitly sets the value of this property to that of the parent.

[number] - An integer between '0' and '100'. A value of '0' produces a monotone voice, while '50' would produce a normal inflection. Pitch ranges greater than 50 create animated voices.

PLAY-DURING

This property specifies a sound to be played while an element's content is rendered.

Mark up

q { play-during: url(accordian.wav) mix }

<q style="play-during: url(accordian.wav) mix">Some text</q>

Possible Values

inherit – Explicitly sets the value of this property to that of the parent.

mix – This value indicates that whatever sound file is to be played for this element will be played with the sound inherited from the parent element's 'play-during' property. If this value is not used, the element's background sound replaces the 'play-during' sound of any parent.

106

repeat – This value indicates that the specified sound will be repeated to fill the time needed to render the element, if it is too short. Otherwise, the sound plays once and then stops. If the 'play-during' sound is longer than the time needed to render the element content it will be clipped.

auto – The 'play-during' sound of the parent element plays only once more.

none – Nothing is played in the background during the element's rendering, not even any parent 'play-during' value. Parent 'play-during' values will resume playing after the element is rendered.

[url] - Indicates the URL to be used as a background sound while the element's content is rendered.

POSITION

This property determines whether normal, relative or absolute positioning methods are used to render the current element box.

Mark up

h2 { display: block; position: absolute; top: 20px; right: 50px; bottom: 20px; left: 50px }

<h2 style="display: block; position: absolute; top: 20px; right: 50px; bottom: 20px; left: 50px">text</h2>

Possible Values

inherit – Explicitly sets the value of this property to that of the parent.

static – This is the default positioning scheme, where elements are rendered in order, as they appear in the document flow. The 'top', 'left', 'right' and 'bottom' properties have no effect if this value is set.

relative – The element's normal document flow position is calculated as if the element had a 'position' value of 'static'. It is then offset from this position according to the 'top' and 'left' properties. Any elements that come after this element will be laid out as if the element had not been offset (a phantom height and width for the element is reserved in the normal document flow.)

absolute – This specifies that the element box be absolutely positioned using the 'top', 'left', 'right' and 'bottom' properties. These values use the element box's containing block as origin. Absolutely positioned elements do NOT exist in the normal document flow like relatively positioned elements are – elements that follow will flow as if the absolutely positioned element does not exist.

fixed - This value behaves like 'absolute' in all respects, but additionally, the positioned element box is fixed with respect to a reference point. In scrolling media, it is in reference to some fixed point on the screen; in paged media (printing) it will be in reference to a point on the page. The positioned element will not move with respect to that stationary point (eg, it will not moved when, say, the screen is scrolled.)

QUOTES

This property determines the type of quotation marks that will be used in a document. One or more quotation mark pairs are given, with the basic quotation characters being the left-most pair. Each subsequent pair represents the quotation characters used at progressively deeper element nesting contexts.

Values of the 'content' property are used to specify where the open/close quotation marks should or should not occur – the "open-quote", "close-quote", "no-open-quote", and "no-close-quote" values. "Open-quote" refers to the left (first) of a given pair of specified quotes, while "close-quote" refers to the second (right) quote character in the pair. Quotes can be skipped at a particular location by using the "no-close-quote" and "no-open-quote" value. In the event that the quote character nesting depth is not covered in the 'quotes' property specification, the last valid quotation pair set should be used.

Mark up

blockquote[lang-=fr] { quotes: "\201C" "\201D" }

blockquote[lang-=en] { quotes: "\00AB" "\00BB" }

blockquote:before { content: open-quote }

blockquote:after { content: close-quote }

Possible Values

inherit – Explicitly sets the value of this property to that of the parent.

none – The 'open-quote' and 'close-quote' values of the 'content' property produce no quotations marks.

([string] - Values for the 'open-quote' and 'close-quote' values of the 'content' property are taken from this list of quote mark pairs. The first or possibly only) pair on the left represents the outermost level of quotation embedding, the pair to the right (if any) is the first level of quote embedding, etc.

[string]) - Values for the 'open-quote' and 'close-quote' values of the 'content' property are taken from this list of quote mark pairs. The first or possibly only) pair on the left represents the outermost level of quotation embedding, the pair to the right (if any) is the first level of quote embedding, etc.

RICHNESS

Mark up

body { richness: 75 }

<body style="richness: 75">text</body>

Possible Values

inherit – Explicitly sets the value of this property to that of the parent.

[number] - This is an integer value between 0 and 100 representing the brightness of the voice. Higher values indicate a brighter voice while lower values create a softer voice.

RIGHT

This describes the horizontal offset for the right edge of the absolutely positioned element box from the right edge of the element's containing block. For relatively positioned boxes, the offsets are relative to where the box would appear normally in the document flow. Positive values are to the left of the parent block's right edge and negative values are to the right.

Mark up

h2 { display: block; position: absolute; top: 20px; right: 50px; bottom: 20px; left: 50px }

<h2 style="display: block; position: absolute; top: 20px; right: 50px; bottom: 20px; left: 50px">content</h2>

Possible Values

inherit – Explicitly sets the value of this property to that of the parent.

auto – Default offset in the regular layout of the page.

[length] – Refers to an absolute distance from the reference containing block. Negative values are allowed.

[percentage] - Refers to a percentage of the height of the parent containing block. If the parent containing block does not have an explicit value, this value is interpreted like 'auto'.

RUBY-ALIGN

This property specifies the horizontal alignment of the Ruby Text (RT) relative to the RUBY element content.

Mark up

ruby { ruby-align: right; ruby-position: above; ruby-overhang: whitespace }

<ruby style="ruby-align: right; ruby-position: above; ruby-overhang: whitespace">Ruby base content<rt>Ruby text</rt></ruby>

Possible Values

auto – The browser determines how the Ruby Text (RT) is to be aligned. Content from Asian character sets will be aligned using the 'distribute-space' method, while non-Asian character content will be aligned using the 'center' method.

left – The left side of the Ruby Text (RT) is aligned with the left side of the Ruby content.

center – The Ruby Text (RT) is centered relative to the Ruby content

right – The right side of the Ruby Text (RT) is aligned with the right side of the Ruby content.

distribute-letter – If the width of the content of the Ruby Text (RT) is less than the width of the RUBY content, the letter-spacing of the RT content is set so that the content is evenly distributed across the width of the RUBY content. For RT widths greater than or equal to the width of the RUBY content, this value is treated like 'center'.

distribute-space – If the width of the content of the Ruby Text (RT) is less than the width of the RUBY content, white space is added to the right and left of the RT content equal to half the kerning value of the RT content. Remaining horizontal space in the RT content is evenly distributed across the width of the RUBY content. For RT widths greater than or equal to the width of the RUBY content, this value is treated like 'center'.

line-edge - If the Ruby Text (RT) is next to or adjacent to a line edge, it is aligned to that edge. Otherwise, it is center aligned. The IE reference is not very clear on what a "line edge" specifically IS.

RUBY-OVERHANG

This property describes how Ruby Text (RT) content will "hang" over other non-ruby content if the RT content is wider than the RUBY content.

Mark up

ruby { ruby-align: right; ruby-position: above; ruby-overhang: whitespace }

<ruby style="ruby-align: right; ruby-position: above; ruby-overhang: whitespace">Ruby base content<rt>Ruby text</rt></ruby>

Possible Values

auto – RT content that is wider than the RUBY content hangs above other text content outside the RUBY.

112

none – RT content that is wider than the RUBY content only hangs above other text content adjacent to the RUBY (not including whitespace outside the RUBY.)

whitespace - RT content that is wider than the RUBY content hangs only above whitespace characters adjacent to the RUBY (not including text outside the RUBY.)

RUBY-POSITION

This property specifies the position of the helper Ruby Text (RT) relative to the Ruby content.

Mark up

ruby { ruby-align: right; ruby-position: above; ruby-overhang: whitespace }

<ruby style="ruby-align: right; ruby-position: above; ruby-overhang: whitespace">Ruby base content<rt>Ruby text</rt></ruby>

Possible Values

above – The Ruby Text (RT) content is located above the RUBY content.

inline - The Ruby Text (RT) content is located in-line with the RUBY content.

SCROLLBAR-3DLIGHT-COLOR

This property describes the color of the outer top and left bevel edges (the normally lighter portion of the "highlights") of the scrollbar arrows and scroll bar slider box portions of a scroll bar

Mark up

body { scrollbar-3dlight-color: #ffff00 }

<body style="scrollbar-3dlight-color: red">content</body>

Possible Values

color - This is a representation of the values for Red/Green/Blue used to determine a final display color.

SCROLLBAR-ARROW-COLOR

This property describes the color of the scrollbar directional arrows of a scroll bar when they are activate-able. When scrllbars appear but are not usable, this property does not control the arrow color in this state.

Mark up

body { scrollbar-arrow-color: green }

<body style="scrollbar-arrow-color: red">content</body>

Possible Values

[color] - This is a representation of the values for Red/Green/Blue used to determine a final display color.

SCROLLBAR-BASE-COLOR

This property describes the color of the button face of the scrollbar arrow widgets, the button face color of the slider widget and half of the dither colors for the scrollbar slider tray

Mark up

body { scrollbar-base-color: blue }

<body style="scrollbar-base-color: blue">content</body>

Possible Values

[color] - This is a representation of the values for Red/Green/Blue used to determine a final display color.

114

SCROLLBAR-DARKSHADOW-COLOR

This property describes the color of the outer bottom and right bevel edges (the normally darker portion of the "shadows") of the scrollbar arrows and scroll bar slider box portions of a scroll bar

Mark up

body { scrollbar-darkshadow-color: #00ffff }

<body style="scrollbar-shadow-color: #cccccc">my content</body>

Possible Values

[color] - This is a representation of the values for Red/Green/Blue used to determine a final display color.

SCROLLBAR-FACE-COLOR

This property describes the color for the button face of the scrollbar arrow widgets, the button face color of the slider widget and the main color of the inactive square at the bottom/right corner of the scrolled box. This property has no effect on the scrollbar tray/track that the scrollbar slider widget travels in

Mark up

body { scrollbar-face-color: red }

<body style="scrollbar-face-color: red">text</body>

Possible Values

[color] - This is a representation of the values for Red/Green/Blue used to determine a final display color.

SCROLLBAR-HIGHLIGHT-COLOR

This property describes the color of the inner top and left bevel edges (the normally darker portion of the "highlights") of the scrollbar arrows, the scroll bar slider box, and half of the dither pattern color of the scrollbar slider tray area (the other half of the dither is taken from the OS default button face color.)

Mark up

body { scrollbar-highlight-color: yellow }

<body style="scrollbar-highlight-color: red">content</body>

Possible Values

[color] - This is a representation of the values for Red/Green/Blue used to determine a final display color.

SCROLLBAR-SHADOW-COLOR

This property describes the color of the inner bottom and right bevel edges (the normally lighter portion of the "shadows") of the scrollbar arrows and scroll bar slider box portions of a scroll bar

Mark up

body { scrollbar-shadow-color: #ff00ff }

<body style="scrollbar-shadow-color:#cccccc">content</body>

Possible Values

[color] - This is a representation of the values for Red/Green/Blue used to determine a final display color.

116

SCROLLBAR-TRACK-COLOR

This property describes the solid color of the scrollbar track

Mark up

body { scrollbar-track-color: #ff00ff }

<body style="scrollbar-track-color: red">content</body>

Possible Values

[color] - This is a representation of the values for Red/Green/Blue used to determine a final display color.

SIZE

This property describes the orientation or dimensions of the page box. The 'size' property classifies a page box so that it is either 'relative' or 'absolute'. 'Absolute' page boxes have a fixed size, whereas 'relative' page boxes will be scaled to fit the target paged media. In the case where a page box is smaller than the intended 'size', CSS2 recommends that it be centered on the page to allow for better alignment of multiple pages.

Mark up

body { size: 8.5in 11in }

<body style="size: 8.5in 11in">test text in the body</body>

Possible Values

inherit – Explicitly sets the value of this property to that of the parent.

auto – This value defines a 'relative' page box, setting the values to the size and orientation of the target page.

portrait – This value defines a 'relative' page box, overriding the target page's current default content orientation, using the typical paradigm where content flows from left to right across the short dimension, and flowing down along the long dimension.

landscape – This value defines a 'relative' page box, overriding the target page's current default content orientation, using the landscape method, where content flows from left to right across the long dimension, and flowing down along the short dimension. This method is often used when a given line will contain larger amounts of content than normal.

[length] - Giving length values for this property creates a page box with fixed dimensions, eg: an 'absolute' page box. Setting only one length value with this value creates a square page box of equal height and width. If two values are specified, the first value represents the page width, and the second represents the page height.

SPEAK

This property specifies whether content will be aurally rendered, and the nature of its rendering. It controls aural rendering in much the same way the 'display' property controls visual rendering.

Mark up

acronym { speak: spell-out }

<acronym style="speak: spell-out">Some Text</acronym>

Possible Values

inherit – Explicitly sets the value of this property to that of the parent.

normal – Uses normal pronunciation rules for the current language to render content.

none – Suppresses/skips aural rendering of the element. No time is taken to render the element. Child elements can override this value.

spell-out – Spells the content one character at a time (useful with acronyms and abbreviations.)

SPEAK-HEADER

This property specifies how often table headers are spoken in relation to their relevant data cells.

Mark up

table { speak-header: once }

<table style="speak-header: once">

Possible Values

inherit – Explicitly sets the value of this property to that of the parent.

once – The table header is spoken once before a series of cells.

always - The table header is spoken every time a relevant data cell is aurally rendered.

SPEAK-NUMERICAL

This property controls how numbers are spoken.

Mark up

.telephone { speak-punctuation: code; speak-numeral: digits }

```
<p>The phone number is <em style="speak-punctuation:
code; speak-numeral: digits">555-1212</em></p>
```

Possible Values

inherit – Explicitly sets the value of this property to that of
the parent.

digits – Speak the number as individual digits.

continuous - Speak the number as a full phrase/word
number. Word representations of numbers are language-
dependent.

SPEAK-PUNCTUATION

This property specifies how punctuation characters are
spoken.

Mark up

.telephone { speak-punctuation: code; speak-numeral:
digits }

```
<p>The phone number is <em style="speak-punctuation:
code; speak-numeral: digits">555-1212</em></p>
```

Possible Values

inherit – Explicitly sets the value of this property to that of
the parent.

code – Punctuation is to be spoken literally.

none - Punctuation is not spoken, but is rendered naturally
as pauses in the rest of the content rendering.

SPEECH-RATE

This property specifies the speaking rate (speed) of the
content.

120

Mark up

strong { speech-rate: fast }

text

Possible Values

inherit – Explicitly sets the value of this property to that of the parent.

x-slow - x-slow: 80 words per minute

slow - slow: 120 words per minute

medium - medium: 180 – 200 words per minute

fast - fast: 300 words per minute

x-fast - x-fast: 500 words per minute

slower - slower: Subtracts 40 words per minute from the current speech-rate faster - faster: Adds 40 words per minute to the current speech-rate

[number] - Positive number indicating speech-rate in words per minute.

STRESS

This is similar to the 'pitch-range' property – it specifies the maximum output height of "local peaks" in the current voice's wave form.

Mark up

body { stress: 75 }

<body style="stress: 75">text</body>

Possible Values

inherit – Explicitly sets the value of this property to that of the parent.

[number] - This is an integer value between 0 and 100. Values are based on language settings (some languages tend to produce higher vocal stresses than others.)

TABLE-LAYOUT

This property controls the layout algorithm used to render table structures.

Using the "automatic" layout algorithm (the table algorithm used by default in most browsers today), all of the table content is required in order to determine the final table layout. For larger quantities of tabular data, this can be MUCH slower than the "fixed" table layout algorithm, especially since more than one analysis might need to be performed on the table data. However, this algorithm does find sufficient minimum and maximum widths for each column, allowing all content in the table's data cells to be appropriately rendered as specified by the author.

Under the "fixed" layout method, the entire table can be rendered once the first table row has been downloaded and analyzed. This can drastically speed up rendering time over the "automatic" layout method, but subsequent cell content may not fit in the column widths provided (the 'clip' and 'overflow' properties control the cell appearance in such a case.)

Mark up

table { table-layout: fixed }

<table style="table-layout: fixed">

Possible Values

inherit – Explicitly sets the value of this property to that of the parent.

auto – Use the automatic table layout algorithm (the method commonly in use in most browsers for table layout.)

fixed - Use the fixed table layout algorithm.

TEXT-ALIGN

The text-align property aligns the text in an element.

Inherited: Yes

Mark up

p {text-align: center}

Possible Values

left – Aligns the text to the left

right – Aligns the text to the right

center – Centers the text

[string] – Specifies a string around which cells in a table column will align. Only applies to table cells. If used for other element types, it will be treated as as "left" or "right" depending on the current language writing direction ("left" for English.)

inherit – Explicitly sets the value of this property to that of the parent.

justify - justified text

TEXT-ALIGN-LAST

This property can be used in conjunction with the 'text-align' property, but the value specified overrides the effects of that property on the horizontal alignment of the last or only rendered line of an element.

Mark up

div { text-align: justify; text-align-last: right}

<div STYLE="text-align: justify; text-align-last: right">this div text is double justified, and the last (or only) line should be right-aligned</div>

Possible Values

left – Left aligns the content on the last or only rendered line of the element.

right – Right aligns the content on the last or only rendered line of the element.

center – Center aligns the content on the last or only rendered line of the element.

inherit – Explicitly sets the value of this property to that of the parent.

auto – Text content on the last line is aligned according to the value of the 'text-align' property, the default text-alignment for the block or its inherited 'text-align' value.

justify - Applies double text justification to the content on the last or only rendered line of the element.

TEXT-AUTOSPACE

This property controls the autospacing and narrow space width adjustment behavior of text. Ideographs are used in many Asian writing systems to represent concepts rather than letters or phonetic strings, and their interpretation may be context-sensitive. This property allows for spacing rules to take into account the presence of ideographs in document content.

Mark up

div { text-autospace: ideograph-numeric; }

This is numeric 123 and English 123 content. Imagine that the English has ideographic characters within, and you would get the idea of this property.

Possible Values

none – No extra spacing is added.

ideograph-alpha – Creates extra spacing between ideographic character groups and non-ideographic text (such as Latin-based, Cyrillic, Greek, Arabic, or Hebrew content.)

ideograph-numeric – Creates extra spacing between groups of ideographic text and numeric characters.

ideograph-parenthesis – Creates extra spacing between a normal (non-wide/half-width) parenthesis and ideograph characters.

ideograph-space - Extends the width of the space character when it is adjacent to ideographs.

TEXT-DECORATION

This property describes the appearance characteristics of text that are not specified with the 'font-style' and 'font-weight' properties. The color of the text-decoration is taken from the 'color' property for the element. The characteristics of this property ARE used by child elements if the parent element is set to block. If this property is specified for an element/section containing no text (like the IMG element) or is empty, this property has no effect. Browsers may treat unknown values as underline.

Mark up

p {text-decoration: underline}

Possible Values

inherit – Explicitly sets the value of this property to that of the parent

none – Defines a normal text

underline – Defines a line under the text

overline – Defines a line over the text

line-through – Defines a line through the text

blink - Defines a blinking text

TEXT-INDENT

This property specifies the horizontal indent from the left side of the current parent Block Element for the first line in the current Block. The indent is only applied at the beginning of the block and not after any intervening line-breaking elements (like BR.)

Note: Negative values are allowed. The first line will be indented to
the left if the value is negative.

Mark up

p {text-indent: 18px}

p {text-indent: -11px}

Possible Values

inherit – Explicitly sets the value of this property to that of the parent

length - Defines a fixed indentation

% - Defines an indentation in % of the width of the parent element

TEXT-JUSTIFY

This property appears to offer a refinement on the "justify" value used in the 'text-align' property. Indeed, the "justify" value must be set for that property for 'text-justify' to have any effect.

'Text-justify' offers a fine level of justification control over the enclosed content, allowing for a variety of sophisticated justification models used in different language writing systems.

Mark up

div { text-align: justify; text-justify: newspaper }

This is "Newspaper" justified content

Possible Values

auto – The browser will determine the appropriate justification algorithm to use

distribute – Justification is handled similarly to the "newspaper" value, but this version is optimized for East Asian content (especially the Thai language.) In this justification method, the last line is not justified.

distribute-all-lines – Behavior and intent for this value is the same as with the "distribute" value, but the last line is also justified.

inter- cluster – Justifies content that does not have any inter-word spacing (such as with many East Asian languages.)

127

inter-ideograph – Used for justifying blocks of ideographic content. Justification is achieved by increasing or decreasing spacing between ideographic characters and words as well.

inter-word – Justification is achieved by increasing the spacing between words. It is the quickest method of justification and does not justify the last line of a content block.

newspaper - Spacing between letters and words are increased or decreased as necessary. The IE reference says "it is the most sophisticated form of justification for Latin alphabets."

TEXT-KASHIDA-SPACE

A "Kashida" is a typographic effect that justifies lines of text by elongating certain characters at carefully chosen points. It is used in Arabic writing systems. This property controls the ratio of kashida expansion to white-space expansion when justifying lines of text in an element. The property can be used with any 'text-justify' justification mode where kashida-style expansion is used ("auto", "distribute", "kashida", and "newspaper".)

Mark up

div { text-align: justify; text-justify: newspaper; text-kashida-space: 75%; }

This is "Newspaper" justified content with text-kashida-space set to "75%".But it won't do anything because the content is English.

Possible Values

inherit – Text is expanded using the text expansion value set on the parent element.

[percentage] - Refers to a ratio bteween kashida expansion and white-space expansion. 0% indicates white-space expansion only, while 100% indicates kashida expansion only.

TEXT-OVERFLOW

Some content in an element may fall outside the element's rendering box for a number of reasons (negative margins, absolute positioning, content exceeding the width/height set for an element, etc.) In cases where this occurs, the 'overflow' (set to "hidden" or "scroll" for this property to have an effect), and 'clip' properties define what content will be visible.

If text is too long for the overflow/clipping area and the content is to be visually clipped, this property allows the clipped content to be visually represented by the string "…" (called an "ellipsis") in the non-clipped area.

This property only applies to text overflow content in the flow of text (horizontal for western text.) To explicitly force an overflow situation, content must be in either a NOBR element or an element with the 'white-space' property set to "nowrap" – otherwise, only a natural non-breaking word existing at the clipping boundary will induce this property to have an ellipsis effect (if the property is thus set.)

The clipped content can still be selected by selecting the ellipsis. When selected, the ellipsis will disappear and be visually replaced by as much of the the text content as is possible to display in the clipping area.

Mark up

div { position: absolute; left: 20px; top: 50px; width: 120px; height: 50px; border: thin solid black; overflow: hidden; text-overflow: ellipsis }

129

```
<div style="position: absolute; left: 20px; top: 50px;
width: 120px; height: 50px; border: thin solid black;
overflow: hidden; text-overflow: ellipsis">

<nobr>This is a NOBR section</nobr>

</div>
```

Possible Values

clip – Clips the viewable content to the area defined by the
rendering box, the 'overflow', and 'clip' property values.

ellipsis - If text content will overflow, display the string
"…" in the visibly-rendered region for content outside the
visible area

TEXT-SHADOW

This property defines one or more comma-separated
shadow effects to be applied to the text content of the
current element. Effects consist of a shadow color, a
maximum blurring radius for the shadow effect and x/y
offset of the shadow effect from the element content.
Multiple effects are applied to the element in the order
specified in the property. Effects can overlap each other,
but they should never overlap the text content.

Mark up

blockquote { text-shadow: blue 2px 2px, red -2px -2px }

Possible Values

inherit – Explicitly sets the value of this property to that of
the parent

none – Defines normal text, with no shadow

[shadow effects] - Specifies one or more comma-separated
shadow effects for the current element. Effects are given

130

as X/Y offsets along with optional shadow-color and blur-radius values

[Shadow-color]: This uses a color to create the shadow effect and may be placed at the beginning or end of the text-shadow effect syntax (see below.) If no color is specified, the value of the 'color' property is used.

[Shadow-offset]: This is given as a pair of length values indicating x- and y- distances to use as offset references from the original text content. The first value specifies the horizontal distance of the offset (positive values are to the right, negative values to the left.) The second value specifies the vertical distance of the offset (positive values are below, negative values are above.)

[Blur-radius]: A length value indicating the boundary of the blurring for the current text-shadow effect.

TEXT-TRANSFORM

This property sets the casing style for a section of text. Content may not be affected if it is not in the ISO 8859-1 character set or does not have an applicable alternate case character to convert to.

Inherited: Yes

Mark up

p {text-transform: uppercase}

Possible Values

inherit – Explicitly sets the value of this property to that of the parent

none – Defines normal text, with lower case letters and capital letters

capitalize – Each word in a text starts with a capital letter

131

uppercase - Defines only capital letters

lowercase - Defines no capital letters, only lower case letters

TEXT-UNDERLINE-POSITION

Sets or retrieves the position of the underline decoration that is set through the textDecoration property of the object.

The auto and auto-pos values apply to this property as of Internet Explorer 6. The default value of this property is auto as of Internet Explorer 6. With Internet Explorer 5.5, the default value of this property is below.

Mark up

p { text-underline-position: above; text-decoration: underline }

content

Possible Values

inherit – Explicitly sets the value of this property to that of the parent

length – Defines a fixed indentation

% - Defines an indentation in % of the width of the parent element

TOP

This describes the vertical offset for the top edge of the absolutely positioned element box from the top edge of the element's containing block. For relatively positioned boxes, the offsets are relative to where the box would appear normally in the document flow. Positive values are below the parent block's top edge and negative values are above.

Mark up

h2 { display: block; position: absolute; top: 20px; right: 50px; bottom: 20px; left: 50px }

<h2 style="display: block; position: absolute; top: 20px; right: 50px; bottom: 20px; left: 50px">content</h2>

Possible Values

inherit – Explicitly sets the value of this property to that of the parent.

auto – Default offset in the regular layout of the page.

[length] – Refers to an absolute distance from the reference containing block. Negative values are allowed.

[percentage] – Refers to a percentage of the height of the parent containing block. If the parent containing block does not have an explicit value, this value is interpreted like 'auto'.

UNICODE-BIDI

Text in some languages flows from right to left, while many other languages flow from left to right. There will inevitably be cases where left to right text and right to left content must be intermingled. Unicode allows for a complex process of determining the directional flow of content based on properties of the characters and content, as well as explicit controls for language "embeddings" and directional overrides. This algorithm should be used with bi-directional content as formatted by CSS. The 'unicode-bidi' and 'direction' properties specify how document content maps to the Unicode algorithm.

Mark up

div { unicode-bidi: embed; direction: rtl }

Bidi content

Possible Values

inherit – Explicitly sets the value of this property to that of the parent.

normal – The element will not open an additional level of embedding. In the case of inline elements, implicit Unicode character ordering will be applied across elements.

embed – Creates an additional explicit Unicode bidi embedding level, with the direction of the content specified by the 'direction' property. Implicit Unicode character ordering is also obeyed.

bidi-override - Creates an additional explicit Unicode bidi embedding level (like the "embed" value), with the direction of the content specified ONLY by the 'direction' property; ordering based on implicit Unicode character properties is not obeyed. This value literally overrides the normal Unicode ordering scheme.

VERTICAL-ALIGN

Element content is typically vertically centered on a rendered line (with extra line-height amounts distributed equally on the top and bottom.) This property allows in-line content boxes to be vertically aligned with respect to several different criteria on a rendered line.

Mark up

img.left { vertical-align: top }

<img style="vertical-align: top" src="image.gif" mce_src="image.gif" >

Possible Values

inherit – Explicitly sets the value of this property to that of the parent.

baseline|middle - baseline – Aligns the baseline of the current element with the baseline of the parent element box. If the current element does not have a baseline, the bottom of the current element's box should be used.

middle – Aligns the vertical midpoint of the current element box with the baseline plus half the x-height of the parent.

top|bottom - top – Aligns the top of the current element with the top of the tallest element on the currently rendered line.

bottom – Aligns the bottom of the current element with the bottom of the lowest element on the currently rendered line.

text-top|text-bottom - text-top – Aligns the top of the current element with the top of the parent element's font.

text-bottom – Aligns the bottom of the current element with the bottom of the parent element's font.

super | sub - super – The baseline of the current element box is aligned to the baseline of other superscripted elements in the parent element's box.

sub – The baseline of the current element box is aligned to the baseline of other subscripted elements in the parent element's box.

[length] - This specifies an exact distance to raise or lower the current element from the default 'baseline' value. Positive values are above the baseline, while negative values are below.

[percentage] - This specifies a distance to raise or lower the current element from the default 'baseline' value. Positive percentages are above the baseline, while negative values are below. The percentage value is relative to the current element's 'line-height' property.

VISIBILITY

This property controls whether the content of an element box is rendered (including the borders and backgrounds.) If an element box is invisible it still affects document layout as if it were visible (to prevent an element box from affecting layout, the 'display' property should be set to 'none'.)

Mark up

p { visibility: hidden }

content

Possible Values

inherit – Explicitly sets the value of this property to that of the

visible – Explicitly sets the value of this property to that of the parent.

hidden – The element box is invisible (completely transparent to content beneath), but still affects document layout flow as if it were visible.

collapse – Unless this value is used in the context of table rows or columns, it will have the same effect as 'hidden'. In the context of tables, spanned cells may be clipped and reacts similar to 'display: none' for the table element.

hide – The element box is invisible (completely transparent to content beneath), but still affects document layout flow as if it were visible.

136

show - The element box is visible.

VOICE-FAMILY

This property indicates a comma-separated, prioritized list (left to right in decreasing priority) of specific and/or generic voice family names. At least one specific or general voice family must be given and it is wise to include a generic voice family as well in case the user does not have any of the specific voices listed. If no match is made, the browser default voice family should be used.

Mark up

strong { voice-family: "Bob Barker", "Monty Hall", male }

Some Text

Possible Values

inherit – Explicitly sets the value of this property to that of the parent.

male - These indicate a generic family of voices, of which any specific voice can be grouped under

female - These indicate a generic family of voices, of which any specific voice can be grouped under

child - These indicate a generic family of voices, of which any specific voice can be grouped under

[specific voice] - This value is a string identifying a specific voice on the user's system. Names containing whitespace should be quoted.

VOLUME

This property refers to the median volume of the current voice. Pitch and inflection variations may vary well above and below this value. The default minimum and maximum values (0/100) should be controllable by the user.

Mark up

body { volume: soft }

<body style="volume: soft">text</body>

Possible Values

Inherit – Explicitly sets the value of this property to that of the parent.

Silent – No sound at all. The time time that would have been taken to aurally render the element is still taken, but no sound is made. Any specified 'pause' properties before/after the element are also rendered. This behavior is different than the 'speak' property being set to none.

x-soft - Same as '0'

soft - Same as '25'

medium - Same as '50'

loud - Same as '75'

x-loud – Same as '100'

[number] – A number between '0' and '100'. '0' represents the minimum audible volume level (not the same effect as "silent") and 100 corresponds to the maximum comfortable volume level.

[percentage] - This measure is relative to the inherited value for the Volume property, and is clipped to the range '0' to '100'.

WHITE-SPACE

Prevent your text from wrapping with nowrap. Note: we have defined the overflow and width CSS attributes, so that you may see nowrap in action.

Mark up

p {white-space: normal}

text

Possible Values

normal – Collapses multiple spaces into one

pre – Does not collapse multiple spaces

nowrap - Does not allow line wrapping without a tag

WIDOWS

This property specifies the minimum number of lines of content for the current element that must be left at the top of a page in a paged display environment.

Mark up

p { widows: 1 }

test text in the paragraph

Possible Values

inherit – Explicitly sets the value of this property to that of the parent.

[integer] - Specifies an integer value representing the minimum number of lines of content that must be left at the top of a page.

WIDTH

This property specifies the width of an element's rendering box for block-level and replaced elements. Negative values are not allowed.

In addition to the 'width' property, two other properties – 'min-width' and 'max-width' – place constraints on the allowed value for an element's rendering box width. The 'width' value is first computed without consideration for these other two properties. If the computed value is greater than the 'max-width' value or less than the 'min-width' value, the width is re-calculated using the 'max-width' or 'min-width' as the new 'width' value.

Mark up

img.class1 { height: 75px; width: 75px }

<img style="height: 75px; width: 75px" src="image.jpg" mce_src="image.jpg">

Possible Values

inherit – Explicitly sets the value of this property to that of the parent.

auto – The width is determinant on the values of other properties.

[length] – Refers to an absolute measurement for the computed element box width. Negative values are not allowed.

[percentage] - Refers to a percentage of the width of the containing

140

WORD-BREAK

This property controls the line breaking behavior within words. It is especially useful in cases where multiple languages are used within an element.

Mark up

div { word-break: keep-all }

Western character set content mixed with a some Asian char content.

Possible Values

normal – Normal line breaking behavior for the language is used.

break-all – Useful where content contains a majority of Asian character set content, to which this value behaves like 'normal'. Non-Asian character set content may be arbitrarily broken across lines.

keep-all - Useful where content contains a minority of Asian character set content, to which content is not broken across lines. For non-Asian character set content, this value behaves like 'normal'.

WORD-SPACING

Specify the exact value of the spacing between your words. Word-spacing works best when pixels are used as the spacing value.

Mark up

p {word-spacing: 30px}

p {word-spacing: -0.5px}

Possible Values

normal – Defines normal space between words

length - Defines a fixed space between words

WORD-WRAP

This property specifies whether the current rendered line should break if the content exceeds the boundary of the specified rendering box for an element (this is similar in some ways to the 'clip' and 'overflow' properties in intent.) This property should only apply if the element has a visual rendering, is an inline element with explicit height/width, is absolutely positioned and/or is a block element.

Mark up

div { word-wrap: break-word }

Here is some content for the div element

Possible Values

normal – Content will exceed the boundaries of the specified rendering box.

break-word - Content will wrap to the next line when necessary, and a word-break will also occur if needed.

WRITING-MODE

This property controls the intrinsic writing direction rendering for a block of content. The default is left-to-right, top-to-bottom common in western languages, but the alternate rendering mode is top-to-bottom, right-to-left which is a common rendering mode used in Asian writing systems. The half-width character rotation effect is not cumulative – it is always rotated with respect to the canvas.

142

Mark up

div { writing-mode: tb-rl; }

Content rendered
vertically

Possible Values

lr-tb – Character glyphs flow one after another from the
source content from left to right, starting from the top of
the element's rendering box. When a new line is started, it
starts below the previous line at the left-hand side of the
element's rendering box.

tb-rl - Character glyphs flow one after another from the
source content from top to bottom, starting from the right
side of the element's rendering box. When a new line is
started, it starts to the left of the previous line at the top
side of the element's rendering box. Full-width characters
are rendered with their top on the same side as top of the
rendering box, and half-width characters (select kana
glyphs and western characters) are rendered rotated 90
degrees clockwise to the original rendering box's
orientation.

Z-INDEX

Positioning of elements in CSS occurs in three dimensions,
not just two. The third dimension is perpendicular to the
screen, giving the screen a sense of depth. Elements can be
overlapped, with "higher", or "closer" elements obscuring
elements that are "lower" or "farther away" (element
transparency becomes an important issue with this
capability.) The placement of elements along this third 'z-
axis' is exactly what this property controls.

Each element's rendering box is automatically assigned an
integer z-index stacking level based on its context in the
document. Boxes with greater z-axis numbers will appear

143

in front of boxes with lower z-axis numbers ('0' and negative numbers are allowed.)

Explicitly setting the 'z-index' property for an element box not only sets its z-position relative to other element boxes in its current context, it also initiates a new stacking context hierarchy, in which the current element box and its child elements partake.

If two or more boxes have the same stacking level within the same context, they are rendered back to front in the order of the document tree. If no 'z-index' property is set for an element box, it inherits the stacking level of its parent element box.

Mark up

h2 { display: block; position: absolute; top: 20px; right: 50px; bottom: 20px; left: 50px; z-index: 3 }

<h2 style="display: block; position: absolute; top: 20px; right: 50px; bottom: 20px; left: 50px; z-index: 3;">content</h2>

Possible Values

inherit – Explicitly sets the value of this property to that of the parent.

auto – The stack level of the current element's box in the current context is the same as that of its parent's. A new local stacking context is not created.

[integer] - This indicates the stack level of the current element's box in the current context. A new local stacking context is created by the current element, with its stack level being 0. Positive and negative integers are allowed.

ZOOM

This property controls the magnification level for the current element. The rendering effect for the element is that of a "zoom" function on a camera. Even though this property is not inherited, it still affects the rendering of child elements.

Mark up

div { zoom: 200% }

This is x2 text

Possible Values

normal – No magnification is applied. The object is rendered as it normally would be.

[number] – Positive floating point number indicating a zoom factor. Numbers smaller than 1.0 indicate a "zoom out" or size reduction effect, while numbers greater than 1.0 indicate a magnifying effect.

[percentage] - Positive floating point number, followed by a percentage character ("%") which indicates a zoom factor. Percentages smaller than 100% indicate a "zoom out" or size reduction effect, while numbers greater than 100% indicate a magnifying effect.

145

www.ingramcontent.com/pod-product-compliance
Lightning Source LLC
Chambersburg PA
CBHW041149050326
40689CB00004B/709